CAULIFLOWER COMFORT FOOD

DELICIOUS LOW-CARB RECIPES
for YOUR FAVORITE
CRAVEABLE CLASSICS

JEANETTE HURT

This book is dedicated to my Uncle Bernie and Aunt Karen.
Your love and support mean the world to me.

Published in the U.S. by:
Ulysses Press
P.O. Box 3440
Berkeley, CA 94703
www.ulyssespress.com

ISBN: 978-1-64604-022-3
Library of Congress Control Number: 2019951367

Printed in Canada by Marquis Book Printing
10 9 8 7 6 5 4 3 2 1

Acquisitions editor: Claire Sielaff
Managing editor: Claire Chun
Editor: Renee Rutledge
Proofreader: Barbara Schultz
Cover design: Rebecca Lown
Cover photographs: casserole © Irina Rostokina/shutterstock.com; pizza © Fascinadora/
   shutterstock.com; spicy cauliflower © Brent Hofacker/shutterstock.com
Interior photos: see page 121
Layout: Jake Flaherty

CONTENTS

Chapter 3
ENTREES 43

Chapter 4
SOUPS, SIDES, AND SALADS 76

Chapter 5
CAULIFLOWER PIZZA AND BREADS 93

Chapter 6
CAULI DESSERTS 110

Whole Roasted Cauliflower, page 9

INTRODUCTION

Meme (from @roxtqt):

Friend: It's called cauliflower. It's not ghost broccoli.

Me: (taking a long drag on my cigarette) Listen, kid, I know what I saw.

All jokes aside, cauliflower remains white hot. Plenty of chain pizzerias offer cauliflower crusts as an option, and if you stroll the aisles of any grocery store, chances are you'll find cauliflower rice, cauliflower tots, and even cauliflower gnocchi in the freezer section. Heck, at some health food stores (and online), you can find cauliflower bread thins and even cauliflower pasta that doesn't contain any regular flours at all.

Gone are the days when cauliflower was a backup to broccoli. This comforting carb replacement speaks keto, does paleo, sneaks in extra servings of veggies, and can be roasted, riced, and baked into everything from bread and pizza to cookies and casseroles.

It's not just turned into breads or added to crackers, it's often used as a total carb replacement. For years, healthy grandmas and moms replaced mashed potatoes with mashed cauliflower, and now, just about everyone knows what they knew back then: It's a vegetable with enough heft to feel like a carb; when it's prepared right, its flavor is mild enough to mimic a carb; and, best of all, when you eat it, you don't miss the carb that it's replacing.

Johanna Israel-Duprey, director of marketing for Hippie Snacks, which makes a line of cauli snacks, says that she realized cauliflower was more than a fad when she saw that California Pizza Kitchen added a cauli crust to their menu. "I think cauliflower works as a carb substitute for so many people because it doesn't actually have to taste like cauliflower," she says. "When you eat the product, you don't feel like you're eating a carb substitute."

This is a trend that seemingly has no end in sight, says Bob Nolan, senior vice president of demand science for Conagra Brands, which makes cauli fries, cauli tots, riced cauli, mashed cauli, and plenty of other cauli products. From 2018 to 2019, the veggie carb category has grown to a whopping $703 million business, with a crazy 83 percent rate of growth. "I've never seen anything growing at this rate, at this size," says Nolan. "We think this is going to be around for a long time. We don't think this is a fad."

"What people love is that it applies to such a broad demographic," says Cybele Pascal, founder of Cybele's Pasta, which makes a cauliflower, parsnip, and lentil pasta. "Athletes love good carbs and high protein, clean eaters and millennials love it, and then you also get moms sneaking vegetables into their kids' diets."

And if you're reading this book, chances are you love cauliflower in all of its wonderful forms and want to learn more about how you can add more of them to your cooking repertoire.

NUTRITION AND BENEFITS

With its great versatility comes an equally impressive amount of nutrients. An entire head of cauliflower contains only 146 calories—a cup contains only 25 calories.

According to the United States Department of Agriculture nutrition database, 1 cup of cauliflower also contains about 2 grams of protein, 24 milligrams of calcium, 16 milligrams of magnesium, 47 milligrams of phosphorus, 320 milligrams of potassium, 52 milligrams of vitamin C, 17 micrograms of vitamin K, nearly .2 micrograms of vitamin B6, and 61 micrograms of folate. That includes 77 percent of your daily vitamin C needs, 20 percent of your daily vitamin K needs, and 10 percent of your vitamin B6 needs.

One cup of cauliflower also contains 3 grams of fiber, and several scientific studies show that a diet rich in fiber from vegetables and fruits can be linked to a lower risk of heart disease, cancer, and diabetes. Fiber can also prevent constipation, and it feeds the healthy bacteria in your gut. It also slows digestion and promotes a feeling of fullness, and that can help in weight loss.

Cauliflower is an amazing source of iron and manganese. It's chock-full of flavonoids. The Centers for Disease Control places cauliflower on its list of "powerhouse fruits and vegetables."

One reason cauliflower is so healthy is that it contains antioxidants that can prevent cell mutations and can reduce oxidative stress from free radicals. In particular, cauliflower is high in two types of antioxidants, glucosinolates, and isothiocyanates, which scientific studies have shown to slow cancer cell growth. Some laboratory studies show that these types of antioxidants can protect against colon, lung, breast, and prostate cancer.

The digestive process of glucosinolates produces the by-product indole-3-carbinol or I3C, an antioxidant that has been shown to reduce the risk of breast and reproductive cancers in women and men.

Another specific antioxidant in cauliflower is sulforaphane, which is a type of isothiocyanate. Some research studies suggest that sulforaphane may inhibit enzymes that cause cancer cells and tumors to grow. It's been studied for its protection against prostate and colon cancers, as well as pancreatic, leukemia, and melanoma cancers. Sulforaphane also might reduce high blood pressure, and it might even have a positive effect on diabetes.

Cauliflower is classified as a cruciferous vegetable—it's in the family with broccoli, cabbage, and Brussels sprouts—and several studies have shown that people who eat more cruciferous vegetables have a lower risk of getting lung and colon cancer.

Various scientific studies show that cauliflower (and other cruciferous vegetables) can slow the rate of cancer cell growth, promote heart health, and reduce obesity. According to a study that was published by the US National Library of Medicine National Institutes of Health, "Brassica (cruciferous) crops have been related to the reduction of the risk of chronic diseases, including cardiovascular diseases and cancer."

Some studies even show that its nutrients remain strong after one year of being in the freezer!

TYPES OF CAULIFLOWER

While white is the most popular color for cauliflower, it can also come in orange, green, and purple; the pointy Romanesco cauliflower comes in a lovely green hue. There are actually 15 different varieties of cauliflower out there, and all of them are quite delicious.

Colored cauliflower offers the same texture and virtually the same taste as regular, white cauliflower. Some people say orange and purple cauliflower taste a little sweeter and a little nuttier than white cauliflower, but other people don't detect any difference at all.

Whether you taste a difference or not, the hued variations are definitely healthier than plain white, as they contain more antioxidants. The purple variations, which range from light violet to deep, dark purple, get their color from an antioxidant called anthocyanin, which is the same antioxidant found in both red wine and red cabbage.

Orange cauliflower gets its coloring from a genetic mutation that allows it to produce more beta carotene, the same substance that gives carrots their color. Beta carotene, when processed in the body, produces more vitamin A.

Green cauliflower, which is sometimes called broccoflower, gets its coloring from the presence of chlorophyll, and it comes in two major styles: regular and Romanesco, which has more pointed, conical florets. Green cauliflower contains more beta carotene than white cauliflower, but less beta carotene than broccoli.

When selecting fresh cauliflower at the supermarket or farmers market, look for all-white florets with few brown spots or discoloration, and look for light-green leaves and stem.

When selecting one of the colorful variations, look for heads that are uniform in color, but don't worry if the hue is light or dark. And, again, look for heads that have as few brown spots or discolorations as possible, and look at the leaves. If the leaves are fresh, not wilted, you've got a fresh head of cauliflower.

Fresh cauliflower keeps on the counter for a day or two, and it keeps in the fridge for about a week.

COOKING CAULIFLOWER

Though my granny loved to boil or steam her cruciferous veggies, cauliflower retains its nutrients better if you roast or sauté it. My favorite method for cooking cauliflower is roasting, but you can sauté and puree it, too.

It's simple to prep the cauliflower for cooking. Use a paring knife to remove any brown spots. Take off any leaves and core the head. What you do after this depends on if you want to cook the cauliflower whole, as pieces, or in riced form (see Basic Cauliflower Recipes below).

Riced cauliflower can be frozen and then ready to use up to a year after freezing, especially if sealed in an airtight container. Roasted cauliflower should be used within three to four days of roasting or within six months if frozen.

EQUIPMENT

As you know, cauliflower can be cooked in many ways. It's helpful to have certain kitchen tools to make doing so as easy as possible.

As roasting is one of the best ways to cook cauliflower, it's important to have a good 18 x 13-inch baking sheet (also called a half sheet pan) or similarly sized roasting pan or baking dish. This is the size I mean in the recipes that call for a baking sheet, roasting pan, or baking dish.

If you don't want to continually line your equipment with parchment paper or aluminum foil, it's a good idea to invest in some silicone baking mats.

Many of the recipes call for extra-virgin olive oil or olive oil spray, and if you don't want to buy the spray, get an olive oil spritzer that you can refill with your favorite type of extra-virgin olive oil. (As a side note, most olive oil sprays are just olive oil sprays, not extra-virgin olive oil sprays, so if you prefer extra-virgin olive oil, then getting a spritzer is a must!)

If you like making your own cauliflower rice, then a food processor is a must. While you can make cauliflower rice by chopping—and chopping and chopping—a head of cauliflower, a food processor makes rice in minutes.

Good, sharp knives are a worthy investment for any home chef, and it's important to keep them sharp. That means, once a year, get them professionally sharpened, and in between, use a knife sharpener and a whetstone to hone them.

COOKING SANITATION AND SAFETY TIPS

The main thing you'll want to do before you begin any recipe is to wash your hands with hot soap and water for at least 30 seconds. Hum the "Happy Birthday" or "ABC" song to yourself.

The second thing you'll want to do is wash your cauliflower, and then pat it dry before cooking it.

If you are cooking a recipe that includes raw meat, please, please wash your hands before and after handling it. And clean all of your cooking surfaces with a mixture of one part bleach and 10 parts water if raw meat or raw meat juice has leaked onto it.

When using sharp knives, lay them flat on the counter, not sharp side up. That's an accident waiting to happen.

BASIC CAULIFLOWER RECIPES

While you can dive right in to any section of this cookbook, these basic cauliflower recipes will be used in several recipes within this book, so it's a good idea to start here or, at least, skim through these recipes first. They're also seriously delicious by themselves.

Each recipe has helpful icons, which will identify the dish as naturally vegan, vegetarian, gluten-free, keto, low-carb, or paleo. That means, for example, that the recipes labeled as gluten-free have no gluten in them. You can easily make other dishes gluten-free if you substitute with gluten-free pie crust or gluten-free flours, but they're not identified as such.

Likewise, if the recipe is labeled keto, it falls into the ketogenic diet practices of eating low carbs and high protein. A low-carb label means the recipe uses very few, if any, sugary or starchy carbs. And the paleo recipes fit into the paleo diet hunters and gatherers used to eat lean meats, fish, fruits and vegetables, nuts and seeds.

Dishes labeled vegan have absolutely no animal products in them, but dishes labeled as vegetarian might have cheese, and some cheeses are made with animal rennet instead of microbial rennet. If you are a vegetarian and prefer microbial rennet, then you might want to choose an American-made Parmesan like those made by Sartori Cheese instead of the Italian-made Parmigiano-Reggiano.

At least half of the recipes are vegan, and at least half of the recipes are gluten-free, and many, many of them are vegetarian, keto, paleo, and low-carb.

But no matter what they're labeled, they're all delicious!

Look for these labels in the recipes:

> V—vegan
>
> VG—vegetarian
>
> GF—gluten-free
>
> K—keto
>
> LC—low-carb
>
> P—paleo

Cauliflower Rice

While most grocery stores now sell riced cauliflower in the frozen produce sections, it's almost as easy to make your own. All you need is fresh cauliflower and a food processor, and you're good to go.

MAKES: 10 to 12 (½-cup) servings | **PREP TIME:** 5 to 10 minutes | **COOK TIME:** None

1 large head of cauliflower (3 to 4 pounds), cut into even chunks and florets, including the stem pieces, leaves removed

1. Fill the food processor with about a quarter of the cauliflower chunks, then pulse to rice-sized pieces, being careful not to pulse until mush.

2. Scoop the processed cauliflower into a medium bowl, then repeat steps 1 and 2 until all of the cauliflower chunks are processed.

3. Use the rice immediately in dishes or store for 3 to 4 days in the refrigerator, or 6 months in the freezer.

NOTE: If you do not have a food processor, use a very sharp chef's knife to slice the cauliflower head into slices, then chop it until it resembles rice.

  If you want to cook the cauliflower rice, simply microwave 1 cup with $\frac{1}{2}$ cup of water in a microwavable bowl on high for 2 to 3 minutes. Or, spray a pan with olive oil spray, heat it for 1 minute, then cook the cauliflower rice, stirring frequently for about 3 to 5 minutes.

Whole Roasted Cauliflower

V GF K LC P

For a recipe so simple and easy to make, the results are dramatic and delicious. It's one of those dishes that you'll likely make over and over again.

MAKES: 8 (½-cup) servings | **PREP TIME:** 5 minutes | **COOKING TIME:** 65 minutes

1 medium head cauliflower (about 1½ to 2 pounds), leaves and 2 inches of core removed

2 tablespoons extra-virgin olive oil

1 teaspoon sea salt

1. Preheat the oven to 400°F.

2. Place the cauliflower in a baking dish lined with aluminum foil. Pour the oil over the cauliflower and massage it into the florets.

3. Sprinkle and massage the sea salt on the florets.

4. Cover the dish with aluminum foil, then bake for 30 minutes.

5. Remove the aluminum foil, bake for 30 more minutes. Broil for 5 minutes to brown the outside of the cauliflower, but don't let it burn.

NOTE: While this basic roasted, whole cauliflower dish tastes amazing as is, if you want a pop of different flavors, you can add 1 teaspoon of garlic powder and/or 1 teaspoon of onion powder, as well as Italian seasoning, Cajun seasoning, or curry powder. Start with just 1 teaspoon and see how you like it. You can also add freshly minced chives, savory, and other herbs—just sprinkle them on the cauliflower after you broil it. And you can't go wrong to sprinkle a tablespoon or two of grated cheese just before broiling.

Roasted Cauliflower Florets

V GF K LC P

This is a great recipe for both special occasions and weeknight desperation dinners. While it's not fast, it's easy and amazingly delicious! For best results, use high heat, but check on your cauliflower because each oven has its own temperature tendencies to run cooler or hotter.

MAKES: 8 to 10 (½-cup) servings | **PREP TIME:** 5 to 10 minutes | **COOK TIME:** 25 to 30 minutes

1 medium head cauliflower (1 ½ to 2 pounds), cored and cut to ½-inch pieces, leaves removed

1 to 2 tablespoons extra-virgin olive oil or extra-virgin olive oil spray

⅛ teaspoon sea salt

⅛ teaspoon freshly ground pepper

1. Preheat the oven to 425°F.

2. Place the cauliflower pieces onto a baking sheet lined with aluminum foil or a silicone baking mat, then brush or spray them with the olive oil. Sprinkle the sea salt and pepper on top.

3. Bake for 12 to 14 minutes, remove from the oven, then use a spatula to flip the pieces over. Spray or brush them with a little more olive oil.

4. Bake for an additional 12 to 14 minutes. The cauliflower will be done when it is lightly browned but not blackened.

Steamed Cauliflower

V GF K LC P

This is a good basic recipe to have on hand if you want to cook cauliflower quickly.

MAKES: 8 (½-cup) servings | **PREP TIME:** 5 minutes | **COOK TIME:** 10 minutes

1 medium head cauliflower (1 ½ to 2 pounds), cored and cut to ½-inch pieces, leaves removed

1 teaspoon sea salt

1. Pour about 1 to 2 inches of water in a stockpot or rice cooker that can be fitted with a steamer basket.

2. Fill the steamer basket with the cauliflower florets.

3. Bring the water to a boil. Then, once the water is boiling, place the steamer basket filled with cauliflower florets on top.

4. Steam the cauliflower for about 6 to 8 minutes. You will know the cauliflower is done when it is tender and you can easily pierce it with a fork. If you want it to mash more easily or if you like it mushy like my granny did, steam it for 10 to 15 minutes.

5. Remove from heat, then season with sea salt.

NOTE: You can also steam your cauliflower in the microwave. Place 2 to 4 tablespoons of water in the bottom of a microwavable bowl that is large enough to contain all the florets, or do this in batches in a smaller bowl. Microwave on high for 3 to 4 minutes.

Chapter 1
BREAKFASTS

Romanesco Cauliflower Corn Pie, page 18

Cauliflower Tofu Scramble

V GF K LC P

This veg-centric scramble boasts both beauty and taste. It's especially delicious at the end of summer and in early fall when both red peppers and tomatoes are in season.

MAKES: 4 servings | **PREP TIME:** 10 minutes | **COOKING TIME:** 10 minutes

1 (14-ounce) container extra-firm tofu

1 teaspoon garlic powder

2 teaspoons sea salt, divided

½ teaspoon freshly ground pepper

olive oil spray

1 cup Roasted Cauliflower Florets (page 10)

1 medium red bell pepper, sliced into 1-inch strips

1 ripe large Roma tomato, diced

3 green onions, diced

2 tablespoons minced cilantro

1. Wrap the tofu in clean paper towels. Place it between two cutting boards and weigh it down with a heavy pot or pan. (You may want to do this in a clean sink because this process will drain the tofu of water, and if you do it on your counter, the water will leak onto the floor.) Let sit for about 10 minutes.

2. Once drained, pat the tofu dry, then rub the outside with garlic powder, 1 teaspoon of sea salt, and pepper, and then dice.

3. Spray a nonstick or cast-iron pan with the olive oil spray, and heat on high heat for 1 minute.

4. Reduce heat to medium-high, add the tofu, sauté for about 5 minutes, then stir in the cauliflower, red pepper, tomatoes, and green onions. Sauté for another 5 minutes.

5. Season with the remaining sea salt, and stir in the cilantro.

Cauliflower Cheese Muffins

VG GF K LC P

These savory muffins can enhance a beautiful brunch, but they're great to serve at a dinner party, too.

MAKES: 12 muffins | **PREP TIME:** 10 minutes | **COOKING TIME:** 20 minutes

1 cup egg whites

1 cup Roasted Cauliflower Florets (page 10)

½ cup almond flour

½ cup coconut flour

1½ cups grated cheddar cheese, divided

1 teaspoon onion powder

1 teaspoon garlic powder

1. Preheat the oven to 350°F.

2. Line a muffin tin with cupcake liners.

3. Whip the egg whites using a mixer until hard peaks form (when you turn the beater upside down, they should hold their shape), about 5 minutes.

4. Meanwhile, puree the cauliflower florets in a food processor. Add the almond and coconut flowers and pulse a few times, then add 1 cup of the cheddar cheese, onion powder, and garlic powder, and pulse a few times until combined.

5. Pour the flour and cheese mixture into a large bowl.

6. Stir one large dollop of whipped egg whites into the flour mixture, then using a spatula, gently fold the rest of the egg whites into the mixture.

7. Gently spoon the batter into the lined muffin tins. Sprinkle the remaining cheddar cheese on top.

8. Bake for 20 minutes until the cheese is slightly brown and the batter no longer jiggles.

NOTE: If you don't have cupcake liners in your cupboard, you can grease the muffin tins with butter, and they should come out rather nicely.

Romanesco Cauliflower Corn Pie

VG LC

This breakfast quiche is not only easy to make but it also freezes well so that you can make it a week or two ahead of entertaining.

MAKES: 4 servings | **PREP TIME:** 10 minutes | **COOKING TIME:** 40 to 45 minutes

1 (9-inch) homemade or store-bought pie crust

6 eggs

½ cup half and half

2 tablespoons minced dried onion

1 teaspoon garlic powder

½ teaspoon sea salt

⅛ teaspoon white pepper

½ cup shredded cheddar cheese

1 cup steamed (page 12) or roasted Romanesco florets (page 10)

1 cup cooked corn

1. Preheat the oven to 400°F.

2. Cover the crust with wax paper or parchment paper and fill with pie weights or 1 cup of dried beans. Bake for 8 to 10 minutes.

3. While the crust is baking, whisk together the eggs, half and half, dried onion, garlic powder, sea salt, and white pepper in a medium bowl.

4. Stir in the cheese, Romanesco florets, and corn.

5. Remove the pie crust from the oven, and pour the egg mixture into the crust.

6. Bake for 30 to 35 minutes or until the pie is no longer jiggly in the middle.

Cauliflower and Caramelized Onion Tart with Fresh Thyme

VG LC

Ah, this tart is inspired by the French countryside and its fields of *choux-fleurs* (cauliflowers). While a completely decadent option for breakfast, with the addition of a soup or salad, you've got yourself a stellar option for dinner, too.

MAKES: 4 servings | **PREP TIME:** 10 minutes | **COOK TIME:** 70 minutes

6 eggs

½ cup heavy cream

½ teaspoon sea salt

⅛ teaspoon white pepper

2 teaspoons extra-virgin olive oil

½ large yellow onion, diced

1 (9-inch) homemade or store-bought pie crust

½ cup shredded mozzarella cheese

1 cup Roasted Cauliflower Florets (page 10)

1 teaspoon fresh thyme leaves

1. Preheat the oven to 400°F.

2. In a medium bowl, whisk together the eggs, heavy cream, sea salt, and white pepper, and set aside.

3. Preheat a large skillet over high heat for 2 minutes. Add the olive oil and heat for 1 minute, then add the onion and sauté for 3 minutes.

4. Reduce the heat to low, stirring every minute or so until completely the onion is caramelized, about 20 minutes.

5. Once the onion is caramelized, remove it from the heat and let it cool slightly.

6. Cover the crust with wax paper or parchment paper, and fill it with pie weights or 1 cup of dried beans. Bake for 8 to 10 minutes.

7. Stir the cheese, roasted florets, fresh thyme, and caramelized onion into the egg mixture. Pour the mixture into the crust.

8. Bake for about 30 to 35 minutes, until the center of the tart is no longer jiggly. Garnish with extra fresh thyme.

Cauliflower "Potato" Pancakes

VG GF K LC P

These pancakes have the texture—and taste—of potato pancakes. They're savory, and they taste great by themselves or topped with a dollop of sour cream and/or apple sauce. Besides being a great breakfast, they're also a great accompaniment to fried or baked fish.

MAKES: 4 servings | **PREP TIME:** 5 minutes | **COOK TIME:** 30 minutes

4 eggs

1 cup Cauliflower Rice (page 7) or frozen cauliflower rice, thawed and drained of excess water

1 cup grated cheddar cheese

4 teaspoons minced dehydrated onion

1 teaspoon garlic powder

1 teaspoon sea salt

olive oil spray

1. Whisk the eggs in a large bowl until frothy.

2. Whisk in the cauliflower rice, cheese, onion, garlic powder, and sea salt until well-combined.

3. Heat the olive oil in a nonstick or cast-iron pan 2 minutes over high heat—until nice and hot.

4. Pour a quarter of the batter into the center of the pan, using a spatula to catch egg dribbles and push them back into the pancake.

5. Cook on high for 2 minutes, then reduce heat to medium and cook for 1 more minute.

6. Flip and cook for another 2 minutes, again using a spatula to push egg dribbles back into the center of the cake.

7. Flip and cook for 1 minute, then flip again and cook for 1 minute.

8. Remove the first pancake from the heat, and repeat the process three more times for remaining cakes.

PREPPING STORE-BOUGHT RICED CAULIFLOWER: If you are using frozen cauliflower, always thaw first. When thawed, use a fine mesh sieve to drain the excess water from the cauliflower rice. Let it sit in the sieve for at least 5 minutes, then press down on the cauliflower rice to get out as much of the water as you can.

Cauliflower and Pumpkin Frittata

VG GF K LC P

This lovely dish is elegant enough to make your brunch guests swoon. As its ingredients can often be found amid the Thanksgiving leftovers, it's also a great Black Friday dish!

MAKES: 4 servings | **PREP TIME:** 10 minutes | **COOK TIME:** 15 minutes

8 eggs

6 tablespoons heavy cream

¾ teaspoon sea salt

½ teaspoon ground nutmeg

¼ teaspoon white pepper

1 tablespoon unsalted butter

1 cup Roasted Cauliflower Florets (page 10)

1 cup cooked cubed pumpkin (or squash or sweet potatoes)

2 tablespoons grated Parmigiano Reggiano cheese, optional

1. Preheat the broiler to high.

2. Whisk the eggs, cream, sea salt, nutmeg, and white pepper in a large bowl until light and fluffy.

3. Preheat an ovenproof pan on the stovetop over high heat for 1 minute. Add the butter and reduce the heat to medium-high.

4. When the butter is melted, stir in the cauliflower and pumpkin. Sauté for 1 to 2 minutes, then add the egg mixture.

5. Using a spatula, fold the egg mixture into the vegetables, and continue to fold and cook the egg mixture for 3 to 4 minutes. Then, stop folding the frittata so that the bottom firms up without burning. Reduce the heat to medium and let sit for 2 to 3 minutes.

6. Sprinkle with cheese, if using, and place the frittata in the oven to broil for about 2 minutes, watching it almost constantly so that it does not burn.

Cauliflower and Potato Hash Tacos

Chapter 2
APPETIZERS

Cauliflower Cheesy Queso, page 36

Spicy Cauliflower "Wings" with Blue Cheese or Bang Bang Sauce

V GF K LC P

Forget chicken. These baked wings have all the spice, and they taste amazing with either blue cheese dressing or Bang Bang Sauce. They're the perfect appetizer for a big game, but they're also a delicious snack!

MAKES: 8 to 10 (½-cup) servings | **PREP TIME:** 10 minutes | **COOK TIME:** 30 minutes

½ cup gluten-free or all-purpose flour

2 teaspoons sea salt

1 teaspoon onion powder

½ teaspoon smoked paprika

½ teaspoon garlic powder

½ teaspoon freshly ground pepper

1 head cauliflower, cut into florets

½ cup plant-based milk

1½ cups gluten-free or regular bread crumbs

olive oil spray

Blue Cheese Sauce (page 28) or Bang Bang Sauce (page 28), to serve

1. Preheat the oven to 425°F. Line a baking sheet with a silicone baking mat or parchment paper.

2. Add the flour, sea salt, onion powder, smoked paprika, garlic powder, and pepper to a medium bowl and stir. Set aside.

3. Dip each floret into the flour mixture, then the plant-based milk. Roll the florets in the bread crumbs, then place on the baking sheet.

4. Spray the florets with the olive oil spray. Bake for 30 minutes until they are nicely brown in color.

5. Serve with blue cheese dressing or Bang Bang Sauce.

NOTE: For an even spicier version, whisk ⅔ cup of Buffalo Sauce (page 32) with ½ cup of plant-based milk batter before baking (you will have some of this mixture leftover).

Blue Cheese Sauce

VG GF K LC P

This is creamy, this is cheesy, and this cools the spice of the wings right down.

MAKES: 6 (1-tablespoon) servings | **PREP TIME:** 5 minutes | **COOK TIME:** None

4 ounces blue cheese, like Gorgonzola

½ cup low-fat buttermilk

1 tablespoon extra-virgin olive oil

1 tablespoon rice wine vinegar or freshly squeezed lemon juice

1 tablespoon Dijon mustard

1 clove garlic

½ teaspoon onion powder

½ teaspoon freshly ground pepper

1 tablespoon minced fresh chives

In a food processor fitted with a standard blade, blend all the ingredients except for the chives for about 2 minutes or until well-mixed. Stir in the chives.

NOTE: If you want this sauce to be thicker, just add another tablespoon or two of blue cheese.

Bang Bang Sauce

V GF K LC P

This easy dipping sauce goes great with baked wings or tossed with roasted cauliflower. It's also great served on the Chickpea and Cauliflower Burgers (page 60).

MAKES: ½ cup, or 4 servings | **PREP TIME:** 5 minutes | **COOK TIME:** None

¼ cup vegan mayonnaise

¼ cup sweet chili sauce

2 tablespoons sriracha

1 teaspoon rice wine or apple cider vinegar

⅛ teaspoon cayenne pepper, optional

Combine all of the ingredients in a small bowl and whisk together.

Cauli-Hummus

GF K LC P

If hummus is your go-to spread for sandwiches, your favorite vegan dip for parties, and one of your favorite snackable treats, then you'll swoon for this cauliflower version.

MAKES: 2 cups | **PREP TIME:** 5 minutes | **COOK TIME:** None

1 (15-ounce) can no-salt or low-salt garbanzo beans

1 cup Cauliflower Rice (page 7)

½ cup tahini

⅓ cup extra-virgin olive oil

2 tablespoons plus ¾ teaspoon fresh lemon juice

1 tablespoon minced garlic

1 tablespoon honey or agave syrup

½ teaspoon sea salt

Puree all ingredients together in a high-speed blender or a food processor fitted with a standard blade until smooth. Serve with chips, pita bread, and/or veggies.

NOTE: To make roasted red pepper cauli-hummus, add ¼ cup of roasted red peppers and ½ teaspoon of smoked paprika to the mix. Use agave syrup instead of honey to make this recipe vegan.

Roasted Cauliflower with Buffalo Sauce

VG GF K LC P

This spiced appetizer will clear your sinuses. It's also tasty and savory enough to serve to company.

MAKES: 8 to 10 (½-cup) servings, 4 to 5 cups | **PREP TIME:** 5 minutes| **COOK TIME:** 10 minutes

1 recipe Roasted Cauliflower Florets (page 10)

1 recipe Buffalo Sauce

2 tablespoons minced fresh parsley or cilantro, to serve

FOR THE BUFFALO SAUCE:

Makes: ½ cup

3 tablespoons unsalted butter, cut into chunks

1 tablespoon apple cider vinegar

2 teaspoons honey

½ teaspoon Worcestershire sauce

¼ teaspoon garlic powder

⅛ teaspoon cayenne pepper

1. Place all of the ingredients for the buffalo sauce into a small pot over medium-low heat. Whisk until the butter is melted.

2. Toss the roasted cauliflower with the buffalo sauce in a large bowl.

3. Plate and garnish with minced herbs to serve.

Caramelized Onion and Cauliflower Dip

VG GF K LC

Forget those cartons of onion dip found next to the cottage cheese in your grocery store or those dried, mix-in packages. This dip is filled with oniony goodness—and it's so easy to make—that you'll never go back to the fake onion dips again.

MAKES: 8 ($\frac{1}{4}$-cup) servings | **PREP TIME:** 5 to 10 minutes | **COOK TIME:** 30 to 35 minutes

2 tablespoons unsalted butter, divided

1 large yellow onion, roughly chopped

1 cup Cauliflower Rice (page 7)

2 cups sour cream

1 tablespoon dried, minced onion

2 teaspoons onion powder

1 teaspoon sea salt

½ teaspoon freshly ground pepper

1. Preheat a large skillet on a stovetop over high heat for 1 to 2 minutes.

2. Melt 1 tablespoon of butter. When the butter has melted, add the onion and reduce the heat to low, stirring constantly for about 3 to 4 minutes.

3. To brown the onion, continue stirring every 2 to 3 minutes until all of the onion pieces get caramelized. This will take 15 to 20 minutes.

4. Add the remaining butter and the riced cauliflower. Cook for another 3 to 4 minutes. Remove from the heat and let cool slightly.

5. Place the caramelized onion and cauliflower mixture into a food processor fitted with a standard blade, pulse for about 2 minutes, then add all the remaining ingredients and pulse until smooth.

Cauliflower Cheesy Queso

V GF K LC P

Queso dips are great to pour over nachos, to use as a dip for tortilla chips, and to serve at a party. Cauliflower adds a richness to this queso dip, but no one will believe they're getting extra veggies as they chow this down.

MAKES: 10 to 12 (⅔-cup) servings | **PREP TIME:** 10 minutes | **COOK TIME:** 15 minutes

1 tablespoon extra-virgin olive oil

½ yellow onion, diced

2 cups cooked Cauliflower Rice (page 7) or frozen cauliflower rice, thawed and drained of excess water

½ roasted poblano or jalapeño pepper, seeds removed, diced

4 cups Béchamel Sauce (page 44)

4 cups shredded Mexican cheese blend or Oaxacan cheese

2 teaspoons ground cumin

2 teaspoons smoked paprika

1 teaspoon sea salt

⅛ teaspoon cayenne pepper

2 tablespoons minced fresh cilantro

salsa, for garnish

1. Preheat a medium pot over medium-high heat for 1 minute. Add the oil and heat for 1 minute.

2. Add the onion and sauté for 3 minutes, or until just it becomes translucent.

3. Add the cauliflower and diced pepper and cook for another 2 minutes. Transfer the mixture to a food processor fitted with a standard blade and puree.

4. Using the same pot, heat the Béchamel sauce over medium heat and stir in the cheese, cumin, paprika, salt, and pepper.

5. Once the cheese is melted, stir in the pureed vegetables. Remove from heat and stir in the cilantro.

6. Transfer to a medium bowl and add a dollop of salsa on top. Serve with chips and/or salsa.

Vegan Cauliflower Queso

V GF K LC P

This isn't exactly as cheesy as a dip made with, well, cheese, but it's cheesy enough in flavor, thanks to the spices and nutritional yeast, and it's savory enough to also please meat eaters.

MAKES: 3½ cups (6 to 8 servings) | **PREP TIME:** 10 minutes | **COOK TIME:** 40 minutes

1 medium head cauliflower, cut into florets

½ large carrot, sliced

4 cloves garlic

½ small yellow onion, sliced

½ poblano pepper, seeds removed and cut into slices

3 tablespoons extra-virgin olive oil

2 teaspoons sea salt, divided

2 tablespoons nutritional yeast

2 teaspoons Cajun seasoning blend

2 teaspoons turmeric powder

1 teaspoon smoked paprika

1 teaspoon ground cumin

½ teaspoon freshly ground pepper

¾ cup nondairy milk

2 tablespoons fresh chopped cilantro and ½ cup pico de gallo, to serve

1. Preheat the oven to 425°F.

2. Place the cauliflower, carrot, garlic, onion, and pepper on a baking sheet lined with parchment paper or a silicone baking mat, brush the vegetables with olive oil, and sprinkle with 1 teaspoon of sea salt. Bake for 30 minutes.

3. Place the cooked vegetables, remaining olive oil, nutritional yeast, remaining spices, and milk into a food processor fitted with a standard blade. Process until completely smooth.

4. Serve with fresh cilantro and pico de gallo, and enjoy with chips.

Gobi Paratha Bread

v

This bread is easy to make, and when served with homemade ketchup or other dipping sauce, it is a fantastic appetizer. But it can also be served for breakfast, and it's a great side dish, especially when making Cauliflower Tikka Masala (page 58).

MAKES: 6 servings | **PREP TIME:** 10 minutes | **COOK TIME:** 40 minutes

FOR THE FILLING:

1½ cups cauliflower florets

½ yellow onion

½ poblano pepper, seeds removed, or 1 small jalapeño pepper, seeds removed

olive oil spray

2 tablespoons fresh cilantro leaves

1 teaspoon grated fresh ginger

½ teaspoon sea salt

¼ teaspoon ground cumin

¼ teaspoon garam masala

¼ teaspoon turmeric powder

olive oil

FOR THE DOUGH:

1½ cups whole wheat flour or gluten-free flour blend plus ½ teaspoon xanthan gum

½ cup water

1 tablespoon extra-virgin olive oil

1. Preheat the oven to 425°F.

2. Spread the cauliflower florets, onion, and pepper onto a baking sheet lined with parchment paper or a silicone baking mat. Spray the vegetables with the olive oil. Bake for 30 minutes, then let cool for 15 minutes.

3. Place the vegetables, cilantro, ginger, sea salt, cumin garam masala, and turmeric into food processor fitted with standard blade, process until smooth.

4. Meanwhile, in a large bowl, whisk together all of the dough ingredients. Form 6 balls. On a lightly floured surface, roll the balls out until they are about 8 to 9 inches in diameter.

5. Place a sixth of the filling in the middle, fold the dough over it, and lightly roll it out. Be very gentle as you roll the dough out; do not stack pancakes because they will stick together.

6. To cook, heat a griddle on the stovetop to high heat, then brush it with olive oil. Cook each pancake for 4 to 5 minutes per side. Serve.

NOTE: Choose the gluten-free flour with the xanthan gum to make this recipe gluten-free.

Crazy Cauli Dip

GF K LC

My sister Karen makes an onion-ranch-bacon-cheddar dip that she calls her "crack" dip—just because it's so addictive. This is my cauliflower version, and it's got my sister's seal of approval.

MAKES: 16 ($\frac{1}{4}$-cup) servings | **PREP TIME:** 10 minutes | **COOK TIME:** 30 to 35 minutes

2 tablespoons unsalted butter or bacon grease, divided

1 large yellow onion, roughly chopped

1 cup Cauliflower Rice (page 7)

2 cups sour cream

8 ounces Neufchâtel cheese or cream cheese

2 tablespoons fresh roughly chopped parsley

2 tablespoons fresh roughly chopped dill

2 tablespoons fresh roughly chopped chives

1 tablespoon onion powder

1 tablespoon garlic powder

1 teaspoon sea salt

½ teaspoon freshly ground pepper

3 pieces of bacon, cooked and crumbled

1 cup shredded cheddar cheese

1. Preheat a large skillet on the stovetop over high heat for 1 to 2 minutes.

2. Add 1 tablespoon of butter or bacon grease. When the butter has melted, add the onions and reduce heat to low, stirring constantly for 3 to 4 minutes.

3. Reduce the stirring to about every 2 to 3 minutes, moving the browning onion around so that all of the onion pieces get caramelized. This will take 15 to 20 minutes.

4. Add the remaining butter or bacon grease and the riced cauliflower. Cook for another 3 to 4 minutes, then remove from heat and let cool slightly.

5. Place the caramelized onion and cauliflower mixture into a food processor fitted with a standard blade, pulse for about 2 minutes, then add all the remaining ingredients except for bacon and cheddar cheese, and pulse until smooth.

6. Add the bacon and cheddar cheese and pulse only 2 or 3 times, until combined.

Cashew Cream Dipping Sauce

V GF K LC P

This vegan dipping sauce is great with tots, wings, and tacos.

MAKES: 1½ cups | **PREP TIME:** 3 to 5 hours | **COOK TIME:** 2 minutes

1 cup unsalted, raw cashews

1 cup water

2 teaspoons nutritional yeast

1 teaspoon onion powder

¼ teaspoon garlic powder

¼ teaspoon sea salt

1. Add the cashews and water to a small bowl and mix. Let sit, covered, for 3 to 5 hours.

2. Puree in a food processor with the remaining ingredients until smooth and creamy.

3. Refrigerate for at least 1 hour before serving.

NOTE: To make this a vegan ranch dipping sauce, add 1 teaspoon agave syrup, ½ teaspoon dried dill, ½ teaspoon dried parsley, and ½ teaspoon dried chives.

Chapter 3
ENTREES

Cauliflower Coconut Tacos, page 65

Béchamel Sauce

VG GF LC P

This basic sauce is in the repertoire for any good French cook, but it is also the base for many dishes in this book, including Cauliflower Mac and Cheese (page 46), Cauliflower Cheesy Queso (page 36), and so much more. Simply put, it is the best white sauce on the planet, and it is so, so easy to make!

MAKES: 4 cups | **PREP TIME:** 5 minutes | **COOK TIME:** 35 minutes, including 20 minutes for infusing

4 cups whole milk

½ yellow onion

1 teaspoon whole peppercorns

1 teaspoon whole cloves

2 bay leaves

2 tablespoons cornstarch or arrowroot powder

2 tablespoons milk, white wine, beer, hard cider, or water

2 tablespoons unsalted butter

1 teaspoon sea salt

1 teaspoon ground white pepper

1. Place the 4 cups of milk, onion, whole peppercorns, whole cloves, and bay leaves into a medium saucepan over medium-high heat. Once it starts simmering, with bubbles forming and a boil just about ready to happen, shut off heat and cover the pan with a lid.

2. Let the infused milk sit for 20 minutes, then strain out the onion, peppercorns, cloves, and bay leaves.

3. Add the cornstarch, or arrowroot powder to a small bowl with the 2 tablespoons of liquid and whisk.

4. Melt the butter over medium heat in the same saucepan, then add the cornstarch or arrowroot paste, whisking quickly. Pour in the infused milk by the half-cup portion, whisking each portion in thoroughly. It should take about 5 minutes to whisk in all of the cornstarch.

5. When the mixture thickens enough to coat the back of a spoon and you can draw your finger on the spoon and leave a path (about 10 minutes), remove the pan from the heat and season with sea salt and ground white pepper.

NOTE: The liquid you use to make a paste with your thickening agent is your choice. Most people use milk or water, but I like the flavor that just a touch of wine, beer, or cider gives the sauce. You can also infuse the sauce with a handful of fresh herbs— thyme and savory work well—but you don't have to. You can make this vegan by using a nondairy milk substitute like almond milk or soy milk.

Cauliflower Mac and Cheese

VG GF

This is pure, unadulterated comfort in a bowl. And you can choose whether to add actual noodles to this or not—it tastes amazing either way.

MAKES: 6 cups with pasta; 4 cups without pasta | **PREP TIME:** 10 minutes | **COOK TIME:** 30 minutes, plus 20 minutes for making pasta

1 cup dry pasta

1 recipe Roasted Cauliflower Florets (page 10)

1 recipe Béchamel Sauce (page 44)

1 teaspoon Dijon mustard

4 cups grated cheese, divided

sea salt and freshly ground white or black pepper, to taste

1. Preheat the oven to 350°F.

2. Cook the pasta according to package directions and set aside.

3. Toss the pasta with the roasted cauliflower and transfer to a ceramic baking dish.

4. Meanwhile, make your Béchamel Sauce, and when the sauce coats the back of the spoon, stir in the Dijon mustard and slowly add 3 cups of cheese by the handful.

5. Season the sauce with sea salt and freshly ground pepper to taste if it needs more seasoning. Pour the cheese sauce over the cauliflower and pasta, and top with remaining cup of cheese.

6. Bake for 30 minutes until browned on top.

NOTE: Even if you use pasta, this can be keto- and paleo-friendly. Cybele's makes a pasta completely from green lentils, cauliflower, and parsnips, and it works exceptionally well in this recipe.

Mac and cheese always tastes better if you use high-quality cheese, and if you use more than one type of cheese. Cheeses that work well include cheddar, Gouda, all Swiss cheeses, and mozzarella. Great (or grate!) add-in cheeses for zips of flavor include Parmigiano-Reggiano, Pecorino Romano, fresh chèvre, and blue cheeses. Parmesan and other hard Italian cheeses taste amazing when sprinkled on top, too.

If you don't want black flecks of pepper to be seen, use white pepper instead.

Quick and Easy, Very Cheesy Cauliflower, Minus the Mac

VG GF K LC

This is a riff on my friend Krissie's recipe. This tastes great by itself, but it also makes for a show-stopping side dish.

MAKES: 8 to 10 (½-cup) servings | **PREP TIME:** 5 to 10 minutes | **COOK TIME:** 25 to 30 minutes

1 medium head cauliflower (1½ to 2 pounds), cut into ½-inch pieces, cored, and leaves removed

1 to 2 tablespoons extra-virgin olive oil or extra-virgin olive oil spray

⅛ teaspoon sea salt

⅛ teaspoon freshly ground pepper

½ small yellow onion

⅓ to 1 cup grated cheddar cheese

1. Preheat the oven to 425°F.

2. Place the cauliflower pieces onto a baking sheet lined with a silicone baking mat or aluminum foil and brush or spray them with the olive oil. Sprinkle the sea salt and pepper on top.

3. Grate the onion on top of the cauliflower. Bake for about 12 to 14 minutes, remove from the oven, then use a spatula to flip onto the other side.

4. Spray or brush with a little more olive oil. Bake for an additional 12 to 14 minutes, until lightly browned but not blackened.

5. Remove the sheet from the oven and turn the broiler on to high heat.

6. Sprinkle cheese on top. Broil for 2 to 3 minutes, until the cheese is gooey and melted onto the vegetables.

NOTE: I personally think, if you use a really good cheddar cheese, all you need is a sprinkling of ⅓ cup. Some of my friends and family disagree with me, so go ahead and add another ⅓ or ⅔ cup of cheese if you really like it cheesy. And don't be afraid to mix and match different cheeses. I think Gouda and cheddar play well together, but if all you have are Swiss and goat cheeses in your fridge, mix and match those, too. And if you are vegan, just use vegan cheese.

Cauliflower Gnocchi

VG LC

These gnocchi boast a soft, pillowy texture that's perfect to sop up any sauce you desire. And, if I do say so myself, they taste better than their potato counterparts.

MAKES: 90 to 100 gnocchi, about 4 servings | **PREP TIME:** 30 minutes | **COOK TIME:** 33 minutes

1 medium head cauliflower, leaves removed, cut into small florets	1⅓ cups gluten-free or all-purpose flour, plus 1 cup for dusting
2 tablespoons extra-virgin olive oil, divided	2 teaspoons sea salt, divided
1 egg	

1. Preheat the oven to 425°F. Spread the florets on a baking sheet fitted with a silicon mat or covered with parchment paper. Drizzle with olive oil and roast for 30 minutes.

2. Remove from heat and let cool to room temperature.

3. Puree florets in a food processor fitted with a standard blade.

4. Add the egg, flour and sea salt, and process until well-blended and the dough begins to pull away from the edges.

5. Form 8 small balls of dough and place them on a counter that's been dusted with 1 cup of flour.

6. Roll each ball out to about 10 inches in diameter, then slice them into 1-inch pieces. Roll each gnocchi across the floured surface using the tines of a fork, gently pressing into each gnocchi as you roll. (This rolling action creates crevices in the gnocchi so that the sauce will better stick to it, but you can skip this step if you so desire.)

7. Place each gnocchi onto a sheet pan. Bring a large pot of water to boil.

8. Carefully drop the gnocchi into the boiling water. Boil for about 3 minutes or until the gnocchi rise to the surface. Drain. Serve with one of the three sauces that follow, or just toss with butter or extra-virgin olive oil and/or cheese.

NOTE: For those who opt for the gluten-free flour, this is one of those gluten-free recipes you can really appreciate. Unlike most gluten-free recipes, it doesn't require extra xanthan gum to thicken it.

Bolognese Sauce

GF K LC P

This is the sauce that dreams are made of. Meaty yet slightly creamy, this sauce dresses up gnocchi, but it tastes equally good on other types of pasta and lasagna.

MAKE: 4 servings, about 4 to 6 cups | **PREP TIME:** 10 minutes | **COOK TIME:** 60 minutes

2 tablespoons extra-virgin olive oil or bacon grease

1 medium yellow onion, diced

1 medium carrot, diced

1 stalk celery, diced

2 pounds ground meat blend of beef, pork, and veal, or 1 pound of beef and 1 pound of pork

1 (28-ounce) can crushed tomatoes

1 cup medium dry red wine

1 (6-ounce) can tomato paste

2 tablespoons sugar

1½ teaspoons sea salt

½ teaspoon freshly ground pepper

½ teaspoon ground cinnamon

½ teaspoon Italian seasoning

2 tablespoons heavy cream (optional)

2 tablespoons minced fresh basil, to serve

1. Preheat a large pot on the stovetop for 1 minute over high heat.

2. Add the olive oil or bacon grease and heat for 1 minute, then add the onion, carrot, and celery and sauté for 5 minutes or until translucent.

3. Add the ground meat and sauté until cooked, about 5 minutes.

4. Add the crushed tomatoes, wine, tomato paste, sugar, sea salt, pepper, cinnamon, and Italian seasoning. Stir until combined, reduce heat to low, and cook for at least 1 hour. Though the sauce will look done after about 20 minutes, if you cook it for the full hour, all of the flavors will fuse and heavenly aromas will waft through your house.

5. Stir in heavy cream, if using. Just before serving, stir in the fresh basil.

NOTE: You can make a cauliflower lasagna by slicing ready-made or homemade cauliflower pizza crusts into slices, and then layering them like lasagna. This bolognese sauce is perfect for lasagna. Stir together 1 container of full-fat ricotta, 1 cup of grated Parmigiano-Reggiano cheese, and an egg to layer with the sauce between layers, and then top with 1 to 2 cups of mozzarella cheese.

Cream Sauce with Fresh Basil and Pancetta

GF K LC P

Oozy-woozy, this creamy dish will put you into a food coma. It's also delicious over gnocchi or pasta, and it's a great dipping sauce for breadsticks, too.

MAKES: 4 servings, about 4 to 6 cups | **PREP TIME:** 10 minutes | **COOK TIME:** 15 minutes

½ pound pancetta, diced

½ cup white wine

4 cups heavy cream

1 cup grated Parmigiano-Reggiano or Asiago cheese

1 cup grated mozzarella

1 teaspoon cornstarch mixed with 1 teaspoon water

1 teaspoon freshly ground pepper

2 tablespoons minced fresh basil

1. Preheat a medium pot on the stovetop over high heat.

2. Add the pancetta and sauté until cooked through, about 5 minutes, then stir in the white wine and reduce until wine is almost cooked off, about another 5 minutes.

3. Reduce heat to medium-high and add the cream, cheeses, and dissolved cornstarch, cooking until the sauce coats the back of a spoon, about 5 minutes.

4. Season with pepper and basil.

5. To serve, toss with gnocchi or pasta.

Fresh Tomatoes, Caramelized Onions, Spinach and Fresh Parmigiano-Reggiano

VG GF K LC P

This delicious sauce tastes of summer, and it's not only great on gnocchi, but it's also delicious when tossed with pasta or even Roasted Cauliflower Florets (page 10).

SERVES: 4 (½-cup servings) | **PREP TIME:** 10 minutes | **COOK TIME:** 30 to 35 minutes

1 tablespoon unsalted butter or extra-virgin olive oil

1 large onion, diced or thinly sliced

4 cups fresh spinach

1 cup grated Parmigiano-Reggiano

1. Preheat a large skillet on the stovetop over high heat for 1 to 2 minutes.

2. Add the butter. When the butter has melted, add the onion and reduce the heat to low, stirring constantly for 3 to 4 minutes.

3. Reduce, stirring every 2 to 3 minutes and moving the browning onion around so that all of the onion pieces get caramelized. This will take 15 to 20 minutes.

4. Add the spinach and sauté for 2 minutes until just cooked.

5. To serve, toss in the cheese and gnocchi or your pasta of choice.

Cauli Tot Casserole

GF K LC P

This is the type of hot dish to take to a church dinner, serve to a neighbor who's stopped by for dinner, or just warm the bellies and hearts of your loved ones. It's a cauli riff on a Midwestern classic.

MAKES: 6 servings | **PREP TIME:** 10 minutes | **COOK TIME:** 30 to 40 minutes

1 pound ground beef

1 small yellow onion, diced

1 (8-ounce) container cheddar cheese spread

¼ cup heavy cream

1 teaspoon garlic powder

1 teaspoon Cajun seasoning

1 teaspoon sea salt

40 cauliflower tots (about 1½ bags of frozen tots or 2 recipes of Cauliflower Tots on page 92)

1½ cups grated cheddar cheese

1. Preheat the oven to 350°F.

2. Preheat a large pan on the stovetop over high heat for 1 minute, then add the beef, sautéing until cooked, about 10 minutes.

3. Add the onion and cook until translucent, about 5 minutes.

4. Stir in the cheese spread, heavy cream, garlic powder, Cajun seasoning, and sea salt, and once thoroughly combined and melted, spread onto a 17 x 11-inch jelly roll pan or medium lasagna pan or casserole dish.

5. Layer cauli tots over the cheese mixture, then sprinkle the cheddar cheese on top.

6. Bake for 25 to 30 minutes, until cheese is melted and oozy.

Aloo Gobi

V GF K LC P

One of my all-time favorite Indian dishes, this is best served with basmati rice or freshly made naan bread. Though this is traditionally made by cooking the vegetables on the stove, I like to roast them beforehand in the oven.

MAKES: 4 servings | **PREP TIME:** 10 minutes | **COOK TIME:** 45 minutes

1 head cauliflower, cut into small florets

3 small potatoes, diced

1 large onion, sliced

1 large tomato, halved

4 to 5 tablespoons extra-virgin olive oil, divided

1 (1-inch) piece of ginger, peeled

1 large clove garlic or 3 small cloves

1 teaspoon cumin seeds

1 teaspoon turmeric powder

1 teaspoon ground cumin

1 teaspoon smoked paprika

1 teaspoon agave syrup, optional

1 teaspoon sea salt

½ teaspoon chili powder or ⅛ teaspoon cayenne pepper, optional

2 tablespoons water, as needed

2 tablespoons minced fresh cilantro, to serve

1. Preheat the oven to 425°F.

2. Place the cauliflower, potatoes, onion, and tomato onto a baking sheet lined with parchment paper or a silicone baking mat. Drizzle with about 2 to 3 tablespoons olive oil.

3. Place the ginger and garlic in a piece of aluminum foil and drizzle with 1 tablespoon olive oil. Bake for 20 minutes, along with the ingredients on the baking sheet. The garlic and ginger will be softened by baking. The tomato will also be softened and slightly charred, the onions will be almost caramelized, and the potatoes and cauliflower will be nicely roasted. Remove from heat and let cool 10 minutes. Separate the tomato from the other vegetables.

4. In a food processor fitted with a standard blade, puree the garlic, ginger, and tomato until smooth. Set aside.

5. Heat a large saucepan over high heat for 2 minutes. Add 1 tablespoon of olive oil and heat for 1 minute.

6. Add the cumin seeds, and as soon as they begin to sizzle, add the remaining spices, the agave syrup, if using, and the ginger-garlic-tomato mixture. Sauté for about 2 minutes.

7. Add the onion, cauliflower, and potatoes and cook for about 5 to 10 minutes, until everything is combined. If the spices seem to be sticking together, add water, 1 tablespoon at a time.

8. Serve with rice and/or naan. Garnish with fresh cilantro.

Grandma's Aloo Gobi

V GF K LC P

My friend Parul's mom makes an aloo gobi that's just the bomb so I had to include the recipe. Usually, she makes it by feel, but she measured everything out for me so that you can make it in your kitchen, too.

MAKES: 4 servings | **PREP TIME:** 10 minutes | **COOK TIME:** 30 to 45 minutes

- 2 tablespoons cooking oil (olive, coconut, or oil of choice)
- 2 dried Indian chili pods
- 1 teaspoon cumin seeds
- 1 teaspoon mustard seeds
- 1 teaspoon Ginger-Garlic Paste
- 1 head cauliflower, cut into florets

- 2 to 3 russet potatoes, peeled and cut into chunks
- 1½ teaspoons turmeric powder
- 1 teaspoon garam masala
- 1 cup peas, optional
- sea salt and freshly ground pepper, to taste

FOR THE GINGER-GARLIC PASTE:

- 1 tablespoon grated ginger or ½ ounce peeled ginger

- 1 tablespoon minced garlic or ½ ounce peeled garlic cloves
- 2 teaspoons extra-virgin olive oil

1. To make the ginger-garlic paste, pulse all of the ingredients together in a high-speed blender until pureed. You will not use all the ginger-garlic paste in this recipe.

2. Heat the oil on the stovetop over high heat in a very large skillet for 1 minute. Add the chili pods, cumin seeds, and mustard seeds and reduce the heat to medium-high, stirring frequently until they become quite aromatic, about 2 minutes.

3. Add the ginger-garlic paste, cauliflower, and potatoes and reduce the heat to low, stirring frequently, about 10 to 15 minutes.

4. Stir in the turmeric, garam masala, and peas, if using, then season with sea salt and pepper to taste. Continue to cook for another 10 to 15 minutes, until all vegetables are tender.

NOTE: You can buy dried chili pods from an Indian grocery or just order online (do a search for "dried Indian chilies," and they will come up). You can substitute with dried serrano chiles, too. You can also buy ginger-garlic paste at Indian grocery stores, or make larger quantities of it. Basically, it is equal parts ginger, garlic, and extra-virgin olive oil, pureed together.

Cauliflower Tikka Masala

V GF K LC P

My kid loves chicken tikka masala so much he's made a song about it. Cauliflower doesn't have quite the same texture as chicken, but it tastes equally good with this vegan tikka masala sauce.

MAKES: 4 servings | **PREP TIME:** 5 minutes | **COOK TIME:** 15 minutes

4 cups roasted or steamed cauliflower florets

FOR THE SAUCE:

1 (13.5-ounce) can light coconut milk

1 (13.5-ounce) can full-fat coconut cream

1 (6-ounce) can tomato paste

½ cup vegetable broth

3 tablespoons agave syrup

1 teaspoon fresh lime juice

1 teaspoon sea salt

1 teaspoon garam masala

1 teaspoon ground cumin

1 teaspoon turmeric powder

1 teaspoon smoked paprika

⅛ teaspoon freshly ground pepper

1. Place all of the ingredients except for cauliflower florets into a large pot on the stovetop over medium high heat. Whisk until smooth and cook until simmering, about 8 to 10 minutes.

2. Add the cauliflower florets, reduce heat to low, and cook for 3 to 4 more minutes. Serve with basmati rice.

Cauliflower Meatloaf

GF K LC

Meatloaf is one of those one-pan, easy weekday meals that everyone in my house loves. It's also one of those meat dishes that can be made healthy-ish with the addition of vegetables. In fact, meatloaves made with more vegetables—instead of just carbs and meat—are juicier and richer tasting, and this meatloaf is no exception to this rule.

MAKES: 8 slices | **PREP TIME:** 10 minutes | **COOK TIME:** 30 to 40 minutes

1 cup cooked Cauliflower Rice (page 7) or frozen cauliflower rice, thawed and drained of excess water

1 medium yellow onion, grated or diced

1 medium carrot, grated or shredded

1 pound lean ground chuck or equal parts chuck, pork, and veal

1 cup gluten-free oats

1 egg, lightly beaten

1 teaspoon sea salt

1 teaspoon onion powder

1 teaspoon garlic powder

1 teaspoon Italian seasoning

½ teaspoon freshly ground pepper

1 (8-ounce) can tomato sauce or 1 cup ketchup

1. Preheat the oven to 375°F.

2. Add the cauliflower, onion, and carrot to a food processor fitted with a standard blade and puree.

3. Transfer the vegetable mixture to a large bowl, add the meat, oats, egg, and seasonings, and stir until well combined.

4. Transfer the mixture to a loaf pan. Top with either tomato sauce or ketchup.

5. Bake for 30 to 40 minutes, until completely cooked to an internal temperature of 155 to 160°F.

Chickpea and Cauliflower Burgers

V GF K LC P

These veggie burgers are easy to make, and they're a great way to use leftover, roasted cauliflower. They're so delicious when served with fresh vegetables—lettuce, tomato, pickles, etc.—on buns or with homemade ketchup.

MAKES: 6 servings | **PREP TIME:** 5 minutes | **COOK TIME:** 6 minutes

2 cups Roasted Cauliflower Florets (page 10)

2 cups chickpea flour

1 small yellow onion

2 cloves garlic

1 ½ teaspoons sea salt

1 teaspoon ground cumin

olive oil spray

1. Place all of the ingredients except for the olive oil spray into a food processor fitted with a standard blade. Process until pureed.

2. Form the dough into six patties.

3. Heat a grill on high. Spray the grill with the olive oil spray, then cook burgers for 3 minutes on each side.

4. Enjoy on buns with fresh vegetables and/or homemade ketchup.

Cauliflower and Cheese Stuffed Tortillas with Cabbage Slaw

GF VG LC

These are a cauliflower riff on a Central American delight called pupusas. Serve them with Cabbage Slaw, extra melted cheese, and/or sour cream.

MAKES: 12 to 14 pupusas | **PREP TIME:** 20 minutes | **COOK TIME:** 20 to 30 minutes

FOR THE DOUGH:

3 cups masa harina

1 teaspoon sea salt

2 cups water

2 tablespoons extra-virgin olive oil

FOR THE FILLING:

1 cup Roasted Cauliflower Florets (page 10) or Steamed Cauliflower (page 12), drained of excess water

1 cup grated cheddar, mozzarella, Monterrey Jack or Oaxacan cheese, plus additional cheese to top, optional

olive oil or olive oil spray for cooking

Cabbage Slaw (page 64), to serve

sour cream, to serve

1. Place the masa harina, sea salt, water, and olive oil in a large bowl and whisk until well combined. Form into 12 to 14 balls about the size of a golf ball. Set aside.

2. In a food processor fitted with a standard blade, chop the cauliflower until almost pureed, and then add cheese, and chop until smooth.

3. To make, roll out 1 dough ball until flat, then place about 1½ tablespoons of the filling in the middle. Fold the dough over, seal, and flatten. If the dough tears, seal and pinch together with oil and a little extra dough and flatten slightly.

4. Repeat and lay the pupusas out on a cookie sheet. You may have a little filling leftover.

5. Brush or spray a griddle with olive oil and set to high. Cook each pupusa for 4 to 5 minutes per side. A standard griddle will fit about 6 to 8 pupusas, but if you are using a sauté pan, try not to crowd it.

6. When done, sprinkle cheese on top, to melt, if you like it cheesy, and serve with Cabbage Slaw and/or sour cream.

Cabbage Slaw or Curtido

GF V LC

This Central American slaw is usually made with white cabbage and white onions, but it also tastes great with red cabbage and red onions.

MAKES: 4 servings | **PREP TIME:** 5 minutes | **COOK TIME:** 20 minutes

3 cups chopped red cabbage

2 medium carrots, grated

½ cup diced red onion

½ cup white vinegar

½ cup water

¼ cup sugar

2 teaspoons sea salt

½ teaspoon dried oregano

1. Place the cabbage, carrots, and red onion in a large bowl. Set aside.

2. Place the vinegar, water, sugar, and sea salt in a small saucepan and bring to a boil. Remove from heat as soon as it reaches a boil, and then pour the liquid over the vegetables and let sit for 10 minutes.

3. Drain, add the dried oregano, and serve.

Cauliflower Coconut Tacos

V GF K LC P

These tasty tacos are great for Taco Tuesdays. Serve with salsa or cashew cream.

MAKES: 10 tacos | **PREP TIME:** 10 minutes | **COOK TIME:** 30 minutes

FOR THE CAULIFLOWER:

½ head cauliflower, cut into florets

¾ cup coconut milk

¾ cup unsweetened coconut shreds

1 teaspoon sea salt

olive oil spray

FOR THE TACOS:

10 flour or corn tortillas

2 cups mixed greens or shredded cabbage

2 regular or pickled jalapeños, diced

1. Preheat the oven to 425°F.

2. Dip the cauliflower florets into the coconut milk, roll them in the coconut shreds, and place them onto a baking sheet lined with parchment paper or a silicone baking mat.

3. Sprinkle the florets with the sea salt and spray with the olive oil spray. Bake for 30 minutes.

4. To assemble the tacos, place a small portion of greens or cabbage on the bottom of each tortilla, and layer with the coconut-covered florets and jalapeño pieces. Top with cashew cream or salsa, if desired.

Salmon and Cauliflower Cakes with Rémoulade Sauce

GF LC

My kid loves this dish, and since it's got both veggies and protein, it's almost a complete meal in and of itself. It's also a great dish to make when you have a can of salmon in your pantry and a cup of leftover, roasted cauliflower.

MAKES: 4 patties | **PREP TIME:** 10 minutes | **COOK TIME:** 8 to 10 minutes

1 cup Roasted Cauliflower Florets (page 10) or Steamed Cauliflower (page 12)

½ small yellow onion

¼ cup gluten-free bread crumbs

1 (6-ounce) no-salt-added can skinless, boneless salmon

1 teaspoon onion powder

1 teaspoon garlic powder

1 teaspoon dried dill or 1 tablespoon fresh dill

½ teaspoon sea salt

½ teaspoon Italian seasoning

¼ teaspoon freshly ground pepper

olive oil spray

Rémoulade Sauce (page 67), to serve

1. Puree the cauliflower florets with the onion and bread crumbs in a food processor fitted with a standard blade.

2. In a large bowl, add the canned salmon, pureed cauliflower and bread crumbs, onion powder, garlic powder, dill, salt, Italian seasoning, and black pepper. Stir together to form 4 patties.

3. Heat the olive oil in a nonstick pan on the stovetop over high heat for 1 minute.

4. Add the cakes, reduce the heat to medium-high, and cook on each side for 3 to 4 minutes. If your pan is large, you can cook all four patties at once, but if it is small, only cook two at a time.

5. Remove from the heat and serve with Rémoulade Sauce.

NOTE: Instead of using roasted cauliflower florets, you can use 1 cup of frozen florets that have been thawed and drained of excess water. The only difference in making them is you will puree the florets by themselves, then strain out excess water. All you have to do is to press down upon them lightly and pour out the water, and then puree them with the bread crumbs and onion.

Rémoulade Sauce

VG GF K LC P

This sauce tastes great with the cauliflower-chickpea cakes, and it is also a fantastic sauce for crab cakes and hush puppies. Use about 1 tablespoon per cauli cake.

MAKES: about ¼ cup sauce | **PREP TIME:** 5 minutes | **COOK TIME:** none

- ¼ cup mayonnaise
- 1 tablespoon ketchup
- 1 tablespoon honey
- 1 teaspoon garlic powder
- 1 teaspoon onion powder

- 1 teaspoon Dijon mustard
- 1 teaspoon dried dill or
- 1 tablespoon fresh dill
- ¼ teaspoon freshly ground pepper

Whisk all of the ingredients together in a small bowl. Serve.

Cauliflower Fried Rice

VG GF K LC P

This is a delicious alternative to regular fried rice, and it's quicker to cook than regular rice, too.

MAKES: 2 servings | **PREP TIME:** 5 minutes | **COOK TIME:** 10 minutes

olive oil spray

1 egg, beaten

1 (12-ounce) bag frozen cauliflower rice, thawed and drained of excess water, or 2¼ cups Cauliflower Rice (page 7)

¼ cup diced red bell pepper

1 green onion, diced

1 tablespoon dried minced onion

1 tablespoon gluten-free soy sauce or tamari

1 tablespoon rice wine vinegar

1 tablespoon agave syrup or honey

2 tablespoons minced fresh cilantro

1. Heat the olive oil spray in a wok or a nonstick cooking pan on the stovetop over high heat for 1 minute, then add the egg and sauté until cooked through. Remove from the heat and dice.

2. Spray additional olive oil spray on a pan and heat over high heat for 1 minute, add the cauliflower rice, and sauté for 2 to 3 minutes.

3. Add the remaining ingredients except for the cilantro and sauté for another 2 to 3 minutes.

4. Stir in the egg and cilantro and cook for 1 minute. Enjoy.

NOTE: To make this vegan, leave out the egg. To make a meatier version, stir in 1 cup of cubed, cooked chicken breast right after you cook the vegetables.

Roasted Cauliflower Florets and Chicken Thighs with Mango Chutney

GF K LC P

This is an easy dinner to make on a busy weeknight, but it's so flavorful, you might also want to make it for company, too.

MAKES: 4 servings | **PREP TIME:** 10 minutes | **COOK TIME:** 30 minutes

1 pound boneless, skinless chicken thighs

1 head cauliflower, cut into bite-size florets

1 (8- to 9-ounce) jar mango chutney

¼ cup extra-virgin olive oil

1 teaspoon turmeric powder

½ teaspoon sea salt

½ teaspoon garam masala

½ teaspoon ground cumin

¼ teaspoon freshly ground pepper

2 tablespoons minced fresh cilantro, to serve

1. Preheat the oven to 425°F.

2. Place the chicken thighs and cauliflower florets onto a baking sheet lined with parchment paper or a silicone baking mat.

3. Add the chutney, olive oil, turmeric powder, sea salt, garam masala, cumin powder, and pepper to a medium bowl, and whisk.

4. Pour the dressing over the cauliflower and chicken. Bake for 30 minutes. The cauliflower will be nicely roasted, and the chicken will be completely cooked, registering 165°F on a meat thermometer with juices running clear.

5. Remove from heat, garnish with cilantro, and serve.

Cauliflower Steaks with Fresh Herbs

V GF K LC P

These cauli-steaks are meaty yet tender to the tooth, and they go great with a side of Mashed Cauliflower with Butter and Chives (page 80) or Cauliflower Rice (page 7).

MAKES: 3 to 4 servings | **PREP TIME:** 5 minutes | **COOK TIME:** 45 minutes

1 whole head cauliflower, leaves removed

3 tablespoons extra-virgin olive oil, divided

½ teaspoon sea salt

½ teaspoon garlic powder, divided, optional

1 tablespoon minced fresh herbs like rosemary, chives, or thyme, to serve

1. Preheat the oven to 425°F.

2. Rub 2 tablespoons of olive oil and the salt over the cauliflower. Roast for 30 minutes, remove from the oven, then cut into steaks. The typical cauliflower head will slice nicely into about 3 to 4 steaks, but sometimes, the end florets will break off—nibble if you're the cook or save for another recipe.

3. Brush the steaks with ½ tablespoon of olive oil, sprinkle with ¼ teaspoon of the garlic powder, return to the oven, and roast for 7 minutes or until just browned.

4. Remove from the oven, flip over, brush with the remaining ½ tablespoon of olive oil, sprinkle with the remaining garlic powder, then roast for 7 more minutes until browned.

5. Remove from the oven, sprinkle with the minced herbs, and serve.

Fried Cauliflower Steaks and Potatoes with Chimichurri Sauce

V GF K LC P

This is meatless potatoes nirvana. The steaks are easy to make, and they taste even more amazing when dipped in Chimichurri Sauce.

MAKES: 3 to 4 servings | **PREP TIME:** 10 minutes | **COOK TIME:** 50 minutes

1 whole head of cauliflower, leaves removed

4 tablespoons extra-virgin olive oil, divided

1 teaspoon sea salt, divided

2 Yukon gold potatoes, peeled and sliced

1 tablespoon fresh herbs of choice, such as chives, dill, or parsley, to garnish

Chimichurri Sauce (page 75), to serve

1. Preheat the oven to 425°F.

2. Rub 2 tablespoons of olive oil and the sea salt over the cauliflower. Roast for 30 minutes, remove from the oven, then cut into steaks. The typical cauliflower head will slice nicely into about 3 to 4 steaks, but sometimes, the end florets will break off—nibble if you're the cook or save for another recipe.

3. Brush the steaks with olive oil (about 1½ teaspoons), return them to the oven, and roast for 7 minutes or until browned. Remove them from the oven, flip them over, and brush them with olive oil (about 1½ teaspoons). Roast for 7 more minutes or until browned.

4. While roasting, heat the remaining tablespoon of olive oil in a nonstick pan on the stovetop over high heat for 1 minute.

5. Add the potatoes and sauté until golden brown, about 3 to 4 minutes.

6. When the steaks are done roasting, sauté them for 30 seconds on each side in the same pan with the potatoes.

7. Sprinkle with the remaining sea salt and fresh herbs as garnish. Serve with Chimichurri Sauce.

Chimichurri Sauce

V GF K LC P

MAKES: 1 cup | **PREP TIME:** 5 minutes | **COOK TIME:** None

½ cup fresh parsley

½ cup fresh cilantro

¼ cup fresh oregano

¼ cup fresh chives

2 tablespoons red wine or
apple cider vinegar

½ medium red bell pepper,
seeds and pith removed

½ jalapeño pepper, seeds
and pitch removed

3 cloves garlic

3 green onions, root end sliced off
(but white and green parts whole)

1-inch piece of fresh ginger root, peeled

¼ cup extra-virgin olive oil

2 tablespoons freshly squeezed lime juice

1 teaspoon sea salt

½ teaspoon freshly ground pepper

Place all sauce ingredients into a high-speed blender or food processor fitted with a standard blade, then process for 1 to 2 minutes, until smooth and creamy.

Chapter 4
SOUPS, SIDES, AND SALADS

Creamy Cauliflower Soup

VG GF K LC P

This is nirvana in a bowl. Rich and creamy, this soup is perfect for warming up on a cold winter's night.

MAKES: 6 servings | **PREP TIME:** 5 minutes | **COOK TIME:** 15 minutes

3 cups Roasted Cauliflower Florets (page 10), plus 2 florets reserved and cut into slices

1 medium yellow onion, roasted

3 cups vegetable stock

1 cup heavy cream

¾ cup freshly grated nutmeg

½ teaspoon sea salt

¼ teaspoon freshly ground pepper

1. In a food processor fitted with a standard blade or a high-speed blender, puree the cauliflower and onion with the vegetable stock until smooth.

2. Pour the mixture into a large stockpot and heat on the stovetop over medium-high heat for about 5 minutes. Stir in the cream and cook until simmering, about 6 to 8 more minutes.

3. Season with the nutmeg, sea salt, and pepper, and cook for an additional 2 minutes.

4. Warm the remaining florets in the microwave for about 30 to 60 seconds, and place a single cut floret into each bowl of soup to serve.

Vegan Cauli Soup

V GF K LC P

If you have leftover roasted cauliflower and some vegetable stock on hand, this is a quick and easy lunch or dinner to make!

MAKES: 4 servings | **PREP TIME:** 5 minutes | **COOK TIME:** 10 minutes

2 cups Roasted Cauliflower Florets (page 10)

1 cup vegetable stock

1 cup soy milk

4 teaspoons nutritional yeast

1 teaspoon garlic powder

2 teaspoons onion powder

1. In a food processor fitted with a standard blade, puree the cauliflower and vegetable stock.

2. Pour the mixture into a medium stockpot, and add the remaining ingredients. Whisk until smooth and cook over medium-high heat until simmering, about 10 minutes.

3. Serve.

Cauliflower Mushroom Risotto

VG GF K LC P

Creamy, mushroomy, ooey-gooey goodness in a bowl—that's what this cauliflower mushroom risotto is. Unlike regular risotto, because this one's made with cauliflower, you don't have to spend hours at the stove, either.

MAKES: 9 (½-cup) servings | **PREP TIME:** 10 minutes | **COOK TIME:** 25 minutes

6 tablespoons unsalted butter, cut into chunks, divided

½ yellow onion, diced

1 shallot, diced

1 (12-ounce) bag frozen cauliflower rice, thawed and drained of excess water, or 1½ cups Cauliflower Rice (page 7)

2 cups shiitake mushrooms, sliced

2 cups cremini mushrooms, sliced

½ cup white wine

1 cup heavy cream

1½ teaspoons sea salt

½ teaspoon freshly ground pepper

¾ cup grated Asiago cheese

½ cup mozzarella or 1 large fresh ball of mozzarella, cut into small chunks

2 tablespoons fresh minced parsley or basil, to garnish

1. Preheat a medium pot on the stovetop over high heat for 2 minutes.

2. Add 4 tablespoons of butter, stirring to melt, then add the onion and shallot, stirring frequently, and sauté until translucent, about 3 to 5 minutes.

3. Add the cauliflower rice, stirring frequently, and sauté for 2 minutes.

4. Add the remaining butter and mushrooms, stirring frequently, and sauté until mushrooms are cooked, about 3 to 5 minutes.

5. Add the wine, cream, sea salt, and pepper, and reduce the heat to medium. Cook for about 10 minutes, stirring frequently, until reduced a little bit.

6. Stir in cheeses until melted, and garnish with fresh herbs.

NOTE: This recipe lends itself to bacon. Replace the unsalted butter with bacon grease, and when you add the cheese, add 4 crumbled strips of bacon.

Mashed Cauliflower with Butter and Chives

VG GF K LC P

At every holiday gathering, my Aunt Judy was required to bring her mashed potatoes. Using her taters as inspiration, I've transformed her dreamy potato dish into an equally dreamy cauliflower recipe.

MAKES: 4 (½-cup) servings | **PREP TIME:** 10 minutes | **COOK TIME:** 15 minutes

3 to 4 cups fresh cauliflower florets (about 1 head) or frozen cauliflower florets, thawed and drained of excess water

4 ounces Neufchâtel cheese (low-fat cream cheese)

4 ounces unsalted butter

¼ cup low-fat sour cream

1 tablespoon minced fresh chives, plus more to garnish

¼ teaspoon sea salt

¼ teaspoon ground white pepper

1 tablespoon butter, to garnish

1. Steam the cauliflower florets for 8 to 10 minutes or until tender.

2. Place the steamed cauliflower, cheese, butter, and sour cream in a food processor fitted with a standard blade and puree until smooth.

3. Pour the mixture into a bowl and stir in the chives, sea salt, and white pepper.

4. Top with the butter and/or a sprinkling of chives.

Granny Hurt's Cream of Cauliflower

VG K GF LC P

My dad hated cabbage so my granny started making her cream of cabbage with cauliflower. This is a creamy, easy side dish.

MAKES: 8 (½-cup) servings | **PREP TIME:** 5 minutes | **COOK TIME:** 30 minutes

1 recipe Béchamel Sauce, made without wine (page 44)

1 (2-pound) head cauliflower, cut into small florets

¼ cup shredded cheese (optional)

1 tablespoon minced fresh Italian parsley or chives, to garnish

1. Preheat the oven to 350°F.

2. Steam the cauliflower florets for 8 to 10 minutes or until tender.

3. Transfer the steamed cauliflower to a medium bowl, and toss with the Béchamel Sauce. Pour the florets and sauce into a casserole dish.

4. Sprinkle with the cheese, if using. Bake for 20 minutes or until slightly browned on top.

5. Sprinkle with fresh herbs.

NOTE: If you want to get fancy, pour the cauliflower mixture into a casserole dish then top with ¾ cup of breadcrumbs and 2 to 3 tablespoons of melted butter. Bake for 20 minutes or until it starts bubbling around the edges.

Roasted Cauliflower Florets with Indian Spices, Goat Cheese, and Fruit

VG K GF LC P

I developed the first incarnation of this recipe for *Chicago Health Magazine*, and each time I've made it since I've tweaked it. Now it tastes ultimately of sweet and savory roasted comfort.

MAKES: 8 (½-cup) servings | **PREP TIME:** 15 minutes | **COOK TIME:** 30 to 35 minutes

1 head cauliflower, cut into 2- to 4-inch pieces, stem and leaves removed

2 green onions, sliced thinly

2 tablespoons minced shallots (about 1 whole shallot)

1 teaspoon minced fresh ginger (about a 2-inch piece)

1 teaspoon turmeric powder

1 teaspoon onion powder

¼ teaspoon freshly ground pepper

¼ teaspoon sea salt

3 tablespoons dried cranberries

3 tablespoons golden raisins

olive oil spray or 2 tablespoons extra-virgin olive oil

2 tablespoons honey

3 to 4 ounces goat cheese, crumbled

1 tablespoon minced fresh cilantro

1. Preheat the oven to 425°F.

2. Line a baking sheet with a silicone mat or aluminum foil. Set aside.

3. Toss the cauliflower, green onions, shallots, ginger, turmeric powder, onion powder, black pepper, and sea salt in a large bowl.

4. Stir in the cranberries and raisins.

5. Spritz the lined cookie sheet with olive oil. Spread the vegetables and fruit onto the cookie sheet without crowding them. Spritz again with olive oil spray. Roast for 12 minutes or until they are browned on one side, remove from the heat, and use a spatula to flip the vegetables and fruit over.

6. Drizzle the vegetables and fruit with honey and return them to the oven to roast for another 12 minutes until they are browned on the second side.

7. Remove from oven and top with goat cheese and cilantro.

8. Return to the oven to broil at high heat for 3 to 5 more minutes, until cheese has melted.

Cauliflower Power Salad

VG GF K LC P

This is a fabulous make-and-take salad that surpasses anything you can find in the deli section of your favorite grocery store. It's perfect for picnics, work lunches, and potluck meals, and it can be made a day or two in advance, as it keeps refrigerated for up to 3 or 4 days.

MAKES: 6 cups | **PREP TIME:** 20 minutes | **COOK TIME:** None

1 medium head cauliflower, florets cut into bite-size pieces, stems diced

½ medium red pepper, diced

½ red onion, diced

½ cup dried cranberries

1 large carrot grated

¼ cup raw sunflower seeds

½ cup sliced almonds

1 tablespoon minced fresh cilantro or Italian parsley

½ cup mayonnaise or vegan mayonnaise

2 tablespoons honey or agave syrup

1 tablespoon Dijon mustard

1 tablespoon olive oil

1 tablespoon rice or apple cider vinegar

1 teaspoon onion powder

1 teaspoon garlic powder

1 teaspoon poppy seeds

¼ teaspoon freshly ground pepper

1. Add the cauliflower, red pepper, red onion, cranberries, carrot, sunflower seeds, almonds, and cilantro or parsley to a large bowl, and toss.

2. Add the mayonnaise or vegan mayonnaise, honey or agave syrup, Dijon mustard, olive oil, rice or apple cider vinegar, onion powder, garlic powder, poppy seeds, and pepper to a small bowl, and whisk.

3. Pour the dressing over the vegetable mixture, stir, and serve.

NOTE: For extra protein, stir in three strips of cooked, crumbled bacon or ½ cup diced, cooked chicken breast.

Cauli-Bouleh

V GF K LC P

This is a cauliflower rice riff on a Middle Eastern dish. It's delicious and refreshing, and it goes great as a side dish when you make the Chickpea and Cauliflower Burgers (page 60).

MAKES: 6 servings | **PREP TIME:** 15 minutes | **COOK TIME:** None

1 head cauliflower, leaves removed	½ red bell pepper, diced, about ½ cup
1 cup loosely packed fresh parsley	4 tablespoons fresh lemon juice
1 cup loosely packed fresh cilantro	1 cup extra-virgin olive oil
1 small onion, diced	1 tablespoon honey
3 Roma tomatoes, diced, about 1½ cups	½ teaspoon sea salt
2 medium cucumbers, diced, about 1 cup	½ teaspoon freshly ground pepper

1. Add the cauliflower to a food processor fitted with a standard blade and chop to finely minced pieces. Transfer to a bowl.

2. Add the parsley and cilantro to the same food processor and chop until finely minced. Stir the herbs into cauliflower.

3. Add the onion, tomatoes, cucumber, and red bell pepper to cauliflower mixture and stir.

4. In a small bowl, whisk together the lemon juice, olive oil, honey, sea salt, and pepper. Toss the dressing onto salad.

5. Drizzle with extra olive oil on top before serving.

Cauliflower Rice Pilaf

GF K LC P

This is a great side dish to serve with chicken, pork, or fish. It's even a terrific—and rather healthy—side dish to serve on Thanksgiving or another special occasion.

MAKES: 6 (½-cup) servings | **PREP TIME:** 10 minutes | **COOK TIME:** 15 minutes

½ cup hot water

¼ cup dried cherries or dried cranberries

2 tablespoons extra-virgin olive oil

½ sweet yellow onion, finely diced

¼ cup shredded carrots

½ cup frozen petite peas

1½ Cauliflower Rice or 1 (12-ounce) bag frozen cauliflower rice, thawed and drained of excess water

1 teaspoon sea salt

2 tablespoons unsalted butter

1 tablespoon minced fresh parsley

1. Pour the hot water over the dried cherries or cranberries, and let sit for 10 minutes to plump up.

2. Heat a large pan on the stovetop over high heat for 1 minute. Add the olive oil and heat for another minute.

3. Add the onion, reduce the heat to medium, then sauté for 2 to 4 minutes, until just starting to brown, then add the carrots, and sauté for another 1 to 2 minutes.

4. Add the peas, sauté for 2 more minutes, then add the riced cauliflower. Sauté another 5 minutes, until everything is cooked through, then stir in the sea salt, butter, and fresh parsley.

Cauliflower "Potato" Salad

GF K LC

This is a cauliflower riff on the world's best potato salad—ensalada Rusa. Ensalada Rusa or "Russian potato salad" is a Spanish tapas dish that is delicious by itself or served alongside crusty bread with which to wipe up any leftover crumbs. (Not that there will not be many, if any, as it's so delicious!)

MAKES: 4 servings, about 2 to 3 cups | **PREP TIME:** 20 minutes | **COOK TIME:** None

1 medium head cauliflower, cut into bite-size pieces, stems removed

2 tablespoons neutral oil like grape seed

¼ teaspoon sea salt

1 cup good-quality mayonnaise

1 (5-ounce) can no-salt-added tuna

1 hard-boiled egg, chopped

1 cup frozen peas, thawed

½ red bell pepper, diced

½ cup diced, cooked carrots

1 Roma tomato, diced

1 tablespoon extra-virgin olive oil

1 tablespoon sherry wine vinegar

sea salt, freshly ground pepper to taste

1. Preheat the oven to 425°F.

2. Add the cauliflower florets to a large bowl, toss with the oil and season with sea salt.

3. Transfer the seasoned cauliflower to a lined baking sheet, then roast for 20 minutes, until just cooked and just starting to brown. Remove from heat, then let cool.

4. Once cooled, transfer the cauliflower to a large bowl and add the mayonnaise, tuna, egg, peas, red pepper, and carrots. Season with sea salt and black pepper to taste.

5. Add the tomatoes, olive oil, and vinegar to a separate bowl, then season with sea salt and black pepper to taste.

6. Pour the tomato mixture on top of the cauliflower salad.

7. Refrigerate for at least 1 hour to let the flavors marinate, then serve.

NOTE: If you prefer potatoes in your potato salad, add 2 cups of cooked, cubed yellow potatoes (like Yukon gold) and ½ cup extra mayonnaise. For the tomato topping, just add 1 extra Roma tomato, 1 extra tablespoon of extra-virgin olive oil, and 1 extra tablespoon of sherry wine vinegar.

Loaded Cauliflower

GF K LC

My friend Susan, who works with dairy farmers, makes a version of this recipe for just about every holiday, and her family raved about it so much that I had to come up with my own recipe (she basically throws ingredients together without measuring). It's the perfect side dish for any occasion.

MAKES: 8 (½-cup) servings | **PREP TIME:** 5 minutes | **COOK TIME:** 40 minutes

1 head cauliflower broken into florets (about 4 cups)

olive oil spray or 1 tablespoon extra-virgin olive oil

1 teaspoon sea salt

1 cup low-fat sour cream

1½ cups shredded cheddar cheese, divided

2 green onions, diced

8 slices bacon, cooked and crumbled

2 tablespoons fresh chives, minced

1. Preheat the oven to 425°F.

2. Line a baking sheet with aluminum foil or parchment paper. Spread the florets onto the parchment sheet. Spray them with olive oil spray or brush with olive oil, then sprinkle sea salt on top.

3. Bake for 35 minutes, until slightly browned and definitely tender. Remove from oven. Let cool about 5 minutes.

4. Transfer the florets to a large bowl and toss with the sour cream, half of the cheese, and all of the green onions.

5. Transfer the mixture to a casserole dish, then top with the bacon and remaining cheddar cheese.

6. Broil on high for about 5 minutes until the cheese has melted and is bubbling, remove from oven, and sprinkle with chives.

Cauliflower Tots

V GF K LC P

This tastes even better than the cauli tots you can find in the produce section of your grocery store. They're perfect to add in casseroles, but they're so good that you and your family will just likely eat them as soon as you take them out of the oven!

MAKES: 6 (4-tot) servings | **PREP TIME:** 15 minutes | **COOK TIME:** 30 minutes

extra-virgin olive oil spray

1½ cups cooked Cauliflower Rice (page 7) or 1 (12-ounce) bag frozen cauliflower rice, thawed and drained of excess water

½ cup cornstarch or arrowroot powder

1 egg

1 teaspoon garlic powder

1 teaspoon onion powder

½ teaspoon sea salt

¼ teaspoon black pepper

¼ teaspoon garlic salt

fresh chives for garnish (about 2 teaspoons)

1. Preheat the oven to 350°F. Line a baking sheet with parchment paper or a silicone baking mat and spray with olive oil.

2. Put the cauliflower rice, arrowroot powder or cornstarch, egg, garlic powder, onion powder, sea salt, and black pepper into a food processor fitted with a standard blade. Pulse the mixture until a dough forms.

3. Scoop the dough out by the teaspoon to form 1-inch balls, and place onto the mat or paper. Spray once more with the olive oil.

4. Bake for 30 minutes, flipping the tots once halfway through the baking time.

5. Remove from the oven, sprinkle with garlic salt and chives, then serve.

Chapter 5
CAULIFLOWER PIZZA AND BREADS

Pesto Pizza with Kale Pesto, Fresh Mozzarella, and Baby Greens, page 101

Cauliflower Breadsticks

VG GF K LC P

This is a rather easy and yummy bread to make. It's cheesy, and it's perfect for dipping into tomato sauce.

MAKES: 6 (2-breadstick) servings | **PREP TIME:** 15 minutes | **COOK TIME:** 25 minutes

olive oil spray

1½ cups cooked Cauliflower Rice (page 7) or 1 (12-ounce) bag frozen cauliflower rice, thawed and drained of excess water

½ cup grated Italian blend like mozzarella, provolone, etc.

1 egg

1 tablespoon minced fresh basil or oregano

1 clove garlic

1 teaspoon dehydrated onion flakes

1 teaspoon garlic powder

1 tablespoon grated Parmigiano-Reggiano or Pecorino Romano cheese

1. Preheat the oven to 425°F. Spray a 9½ x 9½-inch baking dish with olive oil spray. Line with parchment paper and spray again.

2. Drain the riced cauliflower in a fine-mesh sieve for at least 5 minutes, pressing down to drain all excess water.

3. In a food processor fitted with a standard blade, puree the rice, Italian cheese blend, egg, basil or oregano, garlic, and onion flakes. After it becomes a ball of dough, press it into the prepared baking dish.

4. Bake for 20 minutes.

5. Spray the dish with the olive oil spray, sprinkle with the garlic powder and grated cheese on top, then place back in the oven to broil for 5 minutes. Remove from the oven, then slice into breadsticks.

Easy-Peasy Cauliflower Pizza Crust

V VG GF LC

Of all the crusts, this tastes the most like regular pizza crust. The cornmeal adds a nice, rustic touch and makes the crust taste so, so good.

MAKES: 1 (12-inch) pizza, about 4 slices | **PREP TIME:** 5 to 10 minutes | **COOK TIME:** 25 minutes (plus 8 to 10 minutes with toppings)

1 teaspoon extra-virgin olive oil

¼ cup plus 1 teaspoon cornmeal

1½ cups Cauliflower Rice (page 7) or about 12 ounces frozen cauliflower rice, thawed and drained of excess water

1 cup shredded mozzarella

¼ cup grated Parmigiano-Reggiano cheese

2 eggs

¼ cup cornstarch

1. Preheat the oven to 425°F.

2. Brush a pizza stone or baking sheet with olive oil, then sprinkle 1 teaspoon of cornmeal on top. Set aside.

3. Place all remaining ingredients into a food processor fitted with a standard blade. Puree until smooth and pulling away from sides of food processor.

4. Form the dough into a ball, then flatten into a disk using your fingers or a rolling pin. If the dough seems too wet, use your hands to work in 1 to 2 more tablespoons of cornstarch.

5. Using your hands and/or rolling pin, roll the dough onto your prepared pizza stone or baking sheet until the crust is about 12 inches in diameter. It should be about ¼ to ⅛ inch thick. Bake for 20 minutes.

6. Remove the pizza stone from the oven, then use two spatulas to gently loosen and then flip the crust onto the other side.

7. Bake for another 5 minutes, then add your sauce and toppings of choice and bake for 8 to 10 more minutes.

Note on Pizzas

Just about every grocery store on the planet now has ready-made pizza crusts in their freezer section. But not everyone can eat these crusts, which often contain dairy and corn. Because of this—and because not every cauli crust is the same—I have created three different crusts. One is an easy-peasy and still cheesy crust, which contains cornmeal and cornstarch. Another is totally keto—and really, really cheesy. And one is vegan. Unless you have a preference, I recommend making each crust to see which one you like the best.

But if you enjoy the ease of ready-made crusts, you can just choose your favorite crust and then make these delicious pizzas with those as well. It's all up to you!

Cauliflower Cheesy Pizza Crust

VG GF K LC

This pizza crust takes a bit more work than the other two crusts, but it's so delicious and cheesy, it's totally worth the work.

MAKES: 1 (12-inch) pizza, about 4 slices | **PREP TIME:** 5 to 10 minutes | **COOK TIME:** 20 minutes (plus 8 to 10 minutes with toppings)

1 (12-ounce) bag frozen cauliflower rice, thawed and drained of excess water, about 1½ cups

1 large egg

1 cup shredded Italian cheese blend (with mozzarella, provolone, etc.)

¼ cup grated Parmigiano-Reggiano cheese

1 tablespoon extra-virgin olive oil, plus more for speading on stone (about 1 to 2 teaspoons)

1. Place a pizza stone in the middle of cold oven. Preheat the oven to 425°F with the pizza stone inside.

2. Put the riced cauliflower into a fine-mesh strainer and press down to release all water. Pressing the cauliflower will take at least 5 minutes.

3. Put the pressed cauliflower, egg, Italian cheese blend, Parmigiano-Reggiano cheese, and 1 tablespoon of olive oil into a food processor fitted with a standard blade. Blend until smooth and pulling away from the edges of the food processor.

4. Form the dough into a ball, then press into the shape of a disk using your fingers.

5. Using oven mitts, carefully remove the pizza stone from the oven. Carefully drizzle 1 to 2 teaspoons of olive oil onto the stone, then place the disk of dough into the middle of the stone.

6. Using your hands and/or a rolling pin, gently roll out the pizza dough to a diameter of about 12 inches. It should be about ¼ to ⅛ inch thick.

7. Place the pizza crust dough into oven, and bake for 15 minutes. Remove from oven. Using two spatulas, gently flip the crust over and bake for 5 more minutes.

8. Remove from the heat, then add your sauce and toppings of choice and bake for 8 to 10 more minutes.

Vegan Cauliflower Pizza Crust

V GF LC

I came up with this pizza crust for my friend's daughter, Lanie, who is allergic to dairy and corn—two ingredients that are found in almost every ready-made cauli crust on the market. This crust is also quite easy to make, which makes it a double win in my book!

MAKES: 1 (12-inch) pizza, about 4 slices | **PREP TIME:** 10 minutes | **COOK TIME:** 20 to 25 minutes (plus 8 to 10 minutes with toppings)

1 cup frozen diced cauliflower, slightly thawed

½ cup buckwheat flour, plus 1 tablespoon for sprinkling on top

½ cup almond meal

¼ cup ground flaxseeds

2 tablespoons extra-virgin olive oil, divided

¾ teaspoon sea salt, divided

1. Preheat the oven to 425°F.

2. Meanwhile, place the cauliflower, ½ cup of buckwheat flour, almond meal, ground flaxseeds, 1 tablespoon of olive oil, and ½ teaspoon of sea salt into a food processor fitted with a standard blade. Process for about 3 minutes, until it forms a solid dough that pulls away from the sides.

3. Dump the dough into a bowl and form into a ball, then flatten into a disk using your fingers.

4. Spread about 1 tablespoon of olive oil onto a pizza stone. Place disk of dough onto the prepared pizza stone.

5. Using your hands and/or a rolling pin, roll out the dough to about a 12-inch diameter. It should be about ¼ to ⅛ inch thick. Sprinkle 1 tablespoon buckwheat flour on top, then sprinkle ¼ teaspoon sea salt on top.

6. Bake for 15 minutes, until the edges start to brown.

7. Remove the pizza stone from the oven. Using two spatulas, loosen the crust and then flip it over to the other side. Bake another 5 to 8 minutes, being careful not to burn. Remove from oven.

8. Spread with sauce and other toppings of choice. Bake for another 5 to 10 minutes, until toppings are cooked.

Quick Pizza Sauce

V GF LC K P

Yes, you can buy ready-made pizza sauce, but they're often salty, and they don't always taste good. This sauce, on the other hand, is quite yummy, so easy, and so, so delicious, you won't ever go back to store-bought sauces.

MAKES: ¾ cup (enough for at least 1 pizza, with some leftover if you like it less saucy) | **PREP TIME:** 5 minutes | **COOK TIME:** None

1 (6-ounce) can tomato paste	½ teaspoon onion powder
½ cup red wine	¼ teaspoon garlic powder
1 teaspoon Italian seasoning blend	¼ teaspoon sea salt
1 teaspoon honey	¼ teaspoon freshly ground pepper

1. Whisk all the ingredients together in a medium bowl.

2. Spread the sauce on pizza crust or just eat out of the bowl with a spoon. It tastes so good you might want to eat it by itself or just dip bread into it.

NOTE: If you do not have Italian seasoning, you can use dried oregano. You can also add 1 teaspoon minced fresh basil if you have it on hand. Use whatever wine you happen to be drinking at the moment or substitute with hard cider.

Kale Pesto Sauce

This zingy sauce isn't just great for pizza—it's also perfect for gnocchi, too!

MAKES: ¾ cup | **PREP TIME:** 5 minutes | **COOK TIME:** None

3 cloves garlic

3 lacinato kale leaves, stems removed

¼ cup basil leaves

¼ cup pine nuts

¼ cup Parmigiano-Reggiano cheese

¼ cup extra-virgin olive oil

Add all of the ingredients to a food processor fitted with a standard blade and puree.

Pesto Pizza with Kale Pesto, Fresh Mozzarella, and Baby Greens

VG GF K LC P

This delicious pizza focuses on yummy green veggies. It's basically a salad on a pizza.

MAKES: 1 whole (12-inch) pizza, about 4 slices | **PREP TIME:** 5 minutes |
COOK TIME: 3 to 5 minutes

- 1 recipe pizza crust of choice
- 1 recipe Kale Pesto Sauce (page 100)
- 2 cups baby greens
- 2 large balls mozzarella, sliced

1. Preheat the broiler to low.

2. Spread the pesto over the cooked pizza crust. Top with baby greens and mozzarella slices.

3. Serve cold or broil for 3 to 5 minutes, until greens are just wilted and mozzarella is just starting to melt.

Cauliflower Pizza with Spinach, Mozzarella, and Cherry Tomatoes

VG GF K P

This is a delicious, vegetarian pizza, and it's best made with farm-fresh tomatoes and baby spinach. It's the perfect summer pizza.

MAKES: 1 (12-inch) pizza, about 4 slices | **PREP TIME:** 5 | **COOK TIME:** 8 minutes

1 recipe cauliflower pizza crust of your choice

1 recipe Quick Pizza Sauce (page 99)

1 cup baby spinach leaves

10 cherry tomatoes, halved

1 cup shredded mozzarella or shredded vegan mozzarella cheese or 1 ball fresh mozzarella, cut into chunks

2 tablespoons extra-virgin olive oil

1 teaspoon sea salt

1. Preheat the oven to 425°F.

2. Brush the cooked crust with olive oil.

3. Spread the sauce on top, sprinkle with spinach, spread out tomatoes, and sprinkle with cheese. Season with sea salt.

4. Bake for 8 minutes or until cheese has just melted.

Pepperoni and Sausage Pizza

GF K LC P

This pizza is a meat lover's dream. Meaty and delicious, it's perfect for a pizza party.

MAKES: 1 (12-inch) pizza, about 4 slices | **PREP TIME:** 5 minutes | **COOK TIME:** 8 minutes

1 recipe cauliflower pizza crust of your choice

1 recipe Quick Pizza Sauce (page 99)

2 cups grated mozzarella cheese

2 tablespoons grated Parmigiano-Reggiano cheese

1 pound Italian sausage, formed into bite-size balls and cooked

10 to 12 slices pepperoni

½ teaspoon dried oregano

1. Preheat the oven to 425°F.

2. Spread the pizza sauce over the cooked crust. Top with the cheeses.

3. Top with sausage balls and pepperoni slices. Sprinkle with oregano.

4. Cook about 5 to 8 minutes, until the pepperoni is cooked and the cheese is melted and bubbly.

NOTE: You can replace the meats with 1½ cups of cooked vegetables or with vegan meats. You can also replace the tomato sauce with 1 cup of barbecue sauce, replace the pepperoni and sausage with 1 cup of cooked, diced chicken, replace the dried oregano with 2 teaspoons of minced fresh cilantro, and add ½ cup pineapple slices and $\frac{1}{4}$ cup sliced red onions for a barbecue chicken pizza. Then, instead of sprinkling the cilantro before you bake, sprinkle it on the pizza after you remove it from the oven.

Cooked Green Vegan Pizza

V GF LC

This is a version that uses cooked veggies instead of raw.

MAKES: 1 (12-inch) pizza, about 4 slices | **PREP TIME:** 5 minutes | **COOK TIME:** 20 minutes

1 Vegan Cauliflower Pizza Crust (page 98)

1 recipe Quick Pizza Sauce (page 99)

1 bunch thin asparagus stalks, about 10 to 12, ends removed

1 medium zucchini, sliced really thin (either in quarters or strips)

1 cup baby spinach

1 bunch fresh basil leaves

2 teaspoons sea salt

1. Preheat the oven to 350°F. Line a baking sheet with parchment paper or a silicone baking mat. Spread the asparagus onto the cooking sheet, spray with olive oil spray, then sprinkle with ¼ teaspoon of sea salt.

2. On another baking sheet lined with parchment paper or a silicone baking mat, spread the zucchini slices or strips, spray with the olive oil, and then sprinkle with ¼ teaspoon sea salt. Bake the zucchini slices for 8 to10 minutes, and bake the asparagus stalks for 15 minutes.

3. Preheat broiler to high. Spread pizza sauce onto crust, then top with vegetables and herbs. Broil for 3 to 4 minutes, then remove from heat and serve.

NOTE: This version also tastes great with 4 ounces of crumbled goat cheese or feta cheese sprinkled on top.

Margarita Pizza with Spinach

VG GF K LC P

A basic margarita pizza is just tomatoes, olive oil, and fresh basil, and while it's good in its own right, it tastes better when you throw in a few handfuls of baby spinach.

SERVES: Makes 1 (12-inch) pizza, about 4 slices | **PREP TIME:** 10 minutes | **COOK TIME:** 8 to 10 minutes

1 recipe pizza crust of choice

2 tablespoons extra-virgin olive oil

1 cup baby spinach leaves

10 cherry tomatoes, halved

½ cup mozzarella or vegan mozzarella cheese or ½ large mozzarella ball, cut into chunks

1 tablespoon minced fresh basil

1. Preheat the oven to 425°F.

2. Brush the cooked pizza crust with the olive oil.

3. Sprinkle the spinach leaves and tomato halves on top.

4. Sprinkle with mozzarella cheese and fresh basil.

5. Bake for 8 to 10 minutes, until the cheese is melted and vegetables are just cooked.

Vegan Cheese and Tomato Pizza

V GF LC

This vegan version of a margarita pizza boasts all of the flavors of the original. It's a worthy addition to your cauliflower pizza repertoire.

MAKES: 1 (12-inch) pizza, about 4 slices | **PREP TIME:** 5 minutes | **COOK TIME:** 8 minutes

1 Vegan Cauliflower Pizza Crust (page 98)

1 recipe Quick Pizza Sauce (page 99)

2 cups vegan mozzarella cheese shreds

2 small Roma tomatoes, sliced thin

2 tablespoons minced fresh basil

1. Preheat the oven to 425°F.

2. Spread the pizza sauce onto the cooked vegan crust.

3. Sprinkle the vegan cheese shreds across the pizza. Lay the tomato slices on top of the cheese, then sprinkle with the minced basil.

4. Bake for 8 minutes or until the cheese is fully melted.

Chapter 6
CAULI DESSERTS

Flourless Chocolate Cauli Cakelettes, page 111

Flourless Chocolate Cauli Cakelettes

VG GF

This lovely dessert is so dense and chocolaty...nobody will realize it contains cauliflower. And if they do, they won't care as they reach for a second helping.

SERVES: 4 to 6, depending on size of the ramekins | **PREP TIME:** 30 minutes | **COOK TIME:** 30 minutes

2 eggs, separated

¾ cup sugar, divided

¼ cup almond flour

1 tablespoon brandy

1 teaspoon vanilla extract

1 cup semisweet or bittersweet chocolate chips

1 stick unsalted butter (½ cup), cut into chunks

¼ cup cooked Cauliflower Rice (page 7) or frozen califower rice, thawed and drained of excess water

whipped cream and berries, to serve

1. Preheat the oven to 350°F.

2. Add the egg yolks, ¼ cup sugar, almond flour, brandy, and vanilla extract to a food processor fitted with a standard blade and puree. Add the cauliflower rice and puree into the egg yolk mixture.

3. Meanwhile, beat the egg whites until stiff peaks form, then add remaining ½ cup sugar (mixture will be glossy).

4. Melt the chocolate in a double boiler over medium heat. Once melted, reduce heat, then add butter one chunk at a time, whisking until completely melted.

5. Once the butter and chocolate mixture is completely melted, remove from heat, and stir in 1 tablespoon of egg yolk mixture to temper.

6. In a large bowl, slowly whisk the chocolate-butter mixture into the egg yolk mixture. Fold in 1 tablespoon of egg-white mixture, then fold in the rest of the egg-white mixture.

7. Divide the batter among six small or four large ramekins. Place the ramekins into a large pan, and fill the pan with water so that it is halfway up the ramekins.

8. Bake for 30 minutes or until the top is completely hard. Remove from oven, and let cool completely. Serve with whipped cream and berries.

Cauliflower Zucchini Chocolate Bread

V GF

While this is called a "bread," it's really more like a cake, and it's a delicious dessert (or breakfast) to make when your neighbor's garden overflows with a bounty of zucchini.

MAKES: about 8 slices | **PREP TIME:** 10 minutes | **COOK TIME:** 45 to 60 minutes

1 teaspoon oil (like coconut or canola) or melted butter

2 cups gluten-free flour, plus 1 tablespoon to flour pan

½ teaspoon xanthan gum

½ cup cocoa powder

1 teaspoon baking powder

½ teaspoon baking soda

½ teaspoon salt

½ teaspoon ground cinnamon

½ cup almond meal

¾ cup cooked Cauliflower Rice (page 7)

6 tablespoons water, divided

2 tablespoons ground flaxseeds

1 cup packed light brown sugar

1 medium zucchini, shredded (about 2 cups)

½ cup unsweetened applesauce

1 teaspoon vanilla extract

1 cup mini chocolate chips

1. Preheat the oven to 350°F. Grease and flour the pan with the oil or butter and 1 tablespoon gluten-free flour.

2. In a large bowl, sift together the gluten-free flour and xanthan gum with the cocoa powder, baking powder, baking soda, salt, and cinnamon. Stir in the almond meal. Set aside.

3. Puree the cauliflower rice plus 2 tablespoons water in a food processor until smooth.

4. In a small bowl, whisk the flaxseeds with the remaining 4 tablespoons of water.

5. Add the cauliflower puree, flaxseed and water mixture, brown sugar, shredded zucchini, applesauce, and vanilla extract to the dry ingredients, and stir until completely combined.

6. Stir in the mini chocolate chips and pour the batter into the prepared pan.

7. Bake for 45 to 60 minutes or until no longer jiggly in the middle.

Carrot Cauli Cake with Cream Cheese Frosting

VG

Sweet, moist, and rich, this carrot-cauli combination takes the cake.

MAKES: 8 slices | **PREP TIME:** 20 minutes (plus another 10 minutes to frost) | **COOK TIME:** 40 to 45 minutes

2 tablespoons melted unsalted butter or oil (coconut or canola), divided

2 tablespoons flour, divided

1½ cups grated carrots, about 2 large carrots

1 cup Cauliflower Rice (page 7)

1 (20-ounce) can pineapple chunks, juice drained

3 eggs

1½ cups packed dark brown sugar

2 tablespoons maple syrup

2 teaspoons vanilla extract

1 stick (½ cup) unsalted butter

1 teaspoon ground cinnamon

1 teaspoon pumpkin pie spice

3 cups all-purpose or gluten-free flour plus 1 teaspoon xanthan gum

1 tablespoon baking powder

1 teaspoon baking soda

FOR THE FROSTING:

2 sticks (1 cup) unsalted butter

2 (8-ounce) packages low-fat cream cheese

2 cups powdered sugar

1 tablespoon vanilla extract

1. Preheat the oven to 350°F. Grease and flour two 9-inch cake pans with 1 tablespoon oil or butter and 1 tablespoon flour in each pan.

2. In a food processor fitted with a standard blade, puree the carrots, cauliflower, and pineapple chunks.

3. Add the eggs, sugar, maple syrup, vanilla extract, butter, cinnamon, and pumpkin pie spice, and mix until well-combined.

4. In a medium bowl, sift together the flour, baking powder, and baking soda, then add the wet mixture to the dry mixture.

5. Divide the batter between two prepared cake pans. Bake for 40 to 45 minutes or until a toothpick stuck in the middle comes out clean. Let cool for at least 30 minutes.

6. While the cakes are cooling, beat all of the frosting ingredients until blended together. Frost the top of first cake, layer with the second cake, and frost the outside of cakes.

NOTE: To make this vegan, use a vegan butter substitute or coconut oil for the cake, and use a vegan butter substitute and vegan cream cheese substitute for the frosting. You can also substitute the cream cheese frosting by just making a vegan buttercream frosting.

Vegan Chocolate Cauliflower Rice Pudding

V GF LC

Yes, this chocolate pudding is healthier for you than a typical rice pudding. But you won't know it, as its rich, divine chocolaty flavor will make you swoon.

MAKES: 4 servings | **PREP TIME:** 5 minutes | **COOK TIME:** 30 minutes

2 cups plus 2 tablespoons soy milk, divided

½ cup granulated sugar

½ cup chocolate chips

½ cup cooked Cauliflower Rice (page 7) or frozen cauliflower rice, thawed and drained of excess water

4 tablespoons cornstarch

3 tablespoons rum

2 tablespoons cocoa powder

1 teaspoon vanilla extract

Nondairy whipping cream, for garnish

1. Bring 2 cups of soy milk and sugar to a boil over medium-high heat, stirring frequently.

2. Meanwhile, microwave the chocolate chips on high for 1 minute until melted.

3. Place the remaining 2 tablespoons of soy milk, cauliflower, cornstarch, rum, cocoa powder, and vanilla into a food processor fitted with a standard blade. Process until pureed and smooth, about 2 minutes.

4. Once the soy milk and sugar begin to boil, whisk the cauliflower mixture into the milk and reduce the heat to medium.

5. Whisk in the melted chocolate and continue stirring until the mixture begins to thicken.

6. Pour the pudding into 4 ramekin dishes. Garnish with nondairy whipping cream.

Cauliflower Chocolate Chip Oatmeal Cookie Bars

VG GF LC

These bar cookies are healthier than regular cookies, but they taste as good as regular cookies and no one will know there's cauliflower in them at all!

MAKES: 28 to 30 cookies | **PREP TIME:** 10 minutes | **COOK TIME:** 30 minutes

1 cup steamed cauliflower florets, thawed, with excess water pressed out and drained

1 stick unsalted butter

2 cups granulated sugar

1 egg

2 tablespoons white rum

2 teaspoons vanilla extract

1¼ cups rolled oats

1 cup almond flour

1 cup gluten-free flour blend

2 teaspoons baking soda

1 teaspoon xanthan gum

2 (12-ounce) packages chocolate chips

½ teaspoon sea salt

1. Preheat the oven to 350°F.

2. Puree the cauliflower florets in a food processor fitted with a standard blade.

3. Add the butter and sugar, and puree until smooth.

4. Add the egg, rum, and vanilla extract, and puree until smooth.

5. In a large bowl, sift together the rolled oats, almond flour, gluten-free flour blend, baking soda, and xanthan gum.

6. Stir in the cauliflower mixture until well-combined.

7. Stir in the chocolate chips

8. Grease a sheet pan with edges (a 12 x 18-inch jelly roll pan works well). Spread the cookie dough onto the pan like you would with brownies. Sprinkle with sea salt.

9. Bake for 30 minutes or until browned around the edges and cooked through in the middle.

10. Let cool, slice, and serve.

CONVERSIONS

VOLUME

U.S.	U.S. Equivalent	Metric
1 tablespoon (3 teaspoons)	½ fluid ounce	15 milliliters
¼ cup	2 fluid ounces	60 milliliters
⅓ cup	3 fluid ounces	90 milliliters
½ cup	4 fluid ounces	120 milliliters
⅔ cup	5 fluid ounces	150 milliliters
¾ cup	6 fluid ounces	180 milliliters
1 cup	8 fluid ounces	240 milliliters
2 cups	16 fluid ounces	480 milliliters

WEIGHT

U.S.	Metric
½ ounce	15 grams
1 ounce	30 grams
2 ounces	60 grams
¼ pound	115 grams
⅓ pound	150 grams
½ pound	225 grams
¾ pound	350 grams
1 pound	450 grams

TEMPERATURE

Fahrenheit (°F)	Celsius (°C)	Fahrenheit (°F)	Celsius (°C)
70°F	20°C	220°F	105°C
100°F	40°C	240°F	115°C
120°F	50°C	260°F	125°C
130°F	55°C	280°F	140°C
140°F	60°C	300°F	150°C
150°F	65°C	325°F	165°C
160°F	70°C	350°F	175°C
170°F	75°C	375°F	190°C
180°F	80°C	400°F	200°C
190°F	90°C	425°F	220°C
200°F	95°C	450°F	230°C

PHOTO CREDITS

pages 15, 35, 41, 63, 71, 85, 89, 91, 105, 110, 113, 115, © Kyle Edwards. Remaining photos from shutterstock.com:

page vi © Nina Firsova
page 7 © Amallia Eka
page 11 © Anna Hoychuk
page 13 © Yala
page 17 © Nataliya Arzamasova
page 21 © Patnaree Asavacharanitich
page 23 © Bartosz Luczak
page 25 © Martha Graham
pages 26, 29, 69, 81 © Brent Hofacker
page 31 © Kiian Oksana
page 33 © Ravsky
page 39 © StockImageFactory.com

page 43 © JeniFoto
page 45 © Olha Afanasieva
page 47 © Liliya Kandrashevich
page 55 © teleginatania
page 61 © Kiian Oksana
page 73 thefoodphotographer
page 76 © Janet Moore
page 92 ©zarzamora
page 95 © RoJo Images
page 103 © Nataliya Arzamasova
page 107 © Elena Veselova
page 119 © MShev

ACKNOWLEDGMENTS

The author would love to thank her expert agent, Marilyn Allen, her amazing editor Claire Sielaff, and the whole team at Ulysses Press, including Renee Rutledge, Claire Chun, and Jake Flaherty. She also owes a debt of gratitude to her husband Kyle and their son, who ate a LOT of cauliflower while she was writing this cookbook.

ABOUT THE AUTHOR

Jeanette Hurt is a professional writer and recipe developer, and an award-winning author of a dozen books. She has written for numerous magazines, websites, and organizations including *Forbes*, *Eating Well*, *Huffington Post*, and *Chicago Health*. She lives in Milwaukee, Wisconsin. You can follow her on Twitter: @byJeanetteHurt.